BUSINESS SOS

PAUL AVINS

Marketing

Sales

Team

Cashflow

PAUL AVINS

Praise for the book from readers on Amazon.co.uk:

"This book is packed full of useful and practical business tips that anyone in business can apply. They are simple and straight forward and help you make more money.

If you only manage to apply a few of them you'll easily make back the cost of the book several fold in no time. A must read for anyone in business, whatever size it is."

— Richard Hillsdon

"Paul's book is written as individual tips that are easy to understand and easy to implement straight away. So many books of this nature are long-winded and ultimately confusing so this was a breath of fresh air. There are some real gems and many ideas that make you think 'why am I not doing that?'

Off the back of the advice in the book I recently contacted my top 20% of clients, just to say hello and received 3 new quote requests straight away. Something that we all should do but how many of us really do it?

All in all, I highly recommend the book for any business owner looking for some fresh ideas to help them generate new leads and sales, to motivate them, to make them assess their team and to kickstart their business."

— N. Douglas

"I've had this book for just over a week now and it's proving to be a real gem! There literally are 173 fantastic business growth tips inside, covering sales, marketing, time, team and much more... And what's also good is that you don't have to read it cover to cover to get the most out of it - you can dip in and out at will depending on what you need help with! Add to this it's written like a workbook with plenty of places requiring the reader to sit and think about the issues and really engage.

To be honest I wish I'd had this book years ago... it's one on those you want to share with so many people - but yet hate to see it out of your own grasp! For only £12.99 this is easily a must read for any business owner - in my opinion it's well worth its weight in gold."

— Rob Jones

"I have a copy of Paul's Book Business SOS.. It is packed full of up to date and relevent information for where the business world finds itself today.

Business Owners, if you are looking for PROVEN, FAST ACTING and RELEVENT ideas to help your business through these tough times, then this is the book for you. Highly recommended."

— I. Dickson

"As a reader of business development and growth books, and a supporter of any thing that follows the KIS principle this book is a winner. Simple straight forward advise in bite sized chunks. Start by dipping in and find the tip that suits you and follow it. It makes more of a difference than you expect. I used promise small and deliver big. Now looking to implement another one to make a solid foundation. Worth x100 more than the cover price, especially if you DO what it says."

— Peronel Barnes

First published in 2009 by Paul Avins Enterprises Ltd

Unit 4, Westbury Court Business Centre

Marsh Gibbon, Oxon OX27 0AD UK

Cover and book designed and branded by Ayd Instone.

www.sunmakers.co.uk

A division of Eldamar ltd. +44(0)1865 779944

ISBN 13: 978-0-9559610-14

Dedication

Writing this book has been challenging at times, and would not have made it into print without the help and support of some exceptionally talented people who have encouraged and pushed me when I needed it.

My thanks go to Sarah for her copywriting and editing skills and to my wife Sue for being so understanding as I took time away from her and JJ to write and to Angela, who keeps me and my businesses on track.

They say behind every great man is a woman and I have been blessed to have three of the best on my team.

I would also like to thank all of my coaching clients and Wealth Club members, too many to mention personally here, for the opportunity to be a part of their lives and businesses. For the learnings and insights they help me to have and for the encouragement to put strategies and ideas from our sessions into print.

Finally I would like to dedicate this book to an amazing person who has been in my every waking thought since passing away in November 2008 – my Mum, Christine Avins.

Her positive, I-can-overcome-anything attitude inspired me so many times in my life, and still does, proving to me that no matter what circumstances we face we always have a choice, so choose to play the game on your terms and win if you can!

I love and miss you so much Mum.

Paul Avins, 2009

"You have to participate

in your own rescue!"

Client Success Stories
using Strategies Covered in this Book

"Paul's marketing coaching has been a journey of huge learning and great results. Our Average Order Value is up over 100% on this time last year and we've only just started. Paul's coaching helps us to grow so we can grow the business."

— Neil & Sue Green (Owners), Westhill Direct

"In sports the best teams have the best coaches and business is no different in my view. In the last year our sales are up 31% over the previous year and Paul has helped train our sales people, and kept them motivated and on track. The results speak for themselves!"

— Chris Lewis (MD), Chris Lewis Fire and Security

"Following Paul's advice we have maintained a positive attitude, we increased our marketing budget and implemented many of his recession beating strategies. Enquiries were up over 100% year on year in January with a conversion rate of 60%. February enquiries are up 30% with an 85% conversion rate so far. (12 Feb 2009)"

— Niall Douglas (MD), Full Circle Travel

"Talking to my Bank Manager the other day about the way my business is moving forward, he remarked, "Well, you've got a good bank, a good accountant, and you're a member of Paul Avins' Wealth Club, so you've got all the elements in place." And it's true – Paul's coaching, and the contacts and support from other Wealth Club members have meant that profits have trebled over the last two years."

— Sarah Williams (MD), Wordsmith™

"Since joining the Oxford Wealth Club I have received new business worth over £20,000 in the first 6 months!"

— Graham Carson, Partner, INCA Accountants

"I was talking with my bank manager today and whilst discussing the virtues of business coaching and networking I said: "Had I known then what I know now I would have looked for a like minded business coach and networking group when I opened my business nearly 4 years ago, and I hope I would have found Paul Avins first!"
— Bryan Baines (MD), Coversure Insurance Services (Oxford)

"£4,000 from 'dormant' customers – Using just one idea from Paul's Recession Beating workshop, I generated over £4,000 in sales from a list of what I thought were 'dormant' customers."
— Hilary Fletcher, Partner, Ecco Shoes (Oxford)

"Since taking Paul's Kick Start Your Sales program in 2008 our sales are up 34% and our profits are up over 30%, and that's in a credit crunch!"
— Christie Bytom (MD), Bytomic Martial Arts

"My business grew from £650,000 to over £3.9 million in just over 3 years! Paul's Sales and Business Coaching has delivered real results for me."
— David Kirby (MD), Concept Plc

"By using Paul's recession beating strategies in October 2008 our business had the best month in its 30 year history, when loads of other companies in our industry were going bust! His ideas work."
— Matthew Wise (MD), Banbury Litho

"In the last 12 months, Paul's coaching has really helped me to think bigger about my business. My profits are now up over 200% on last year and we are still growing – you can't argue with results like that!"
— Jill Treloggen (MD), Jill Treloggen Interiors

Contents

*"Our own success, to be real, must
contribute to the success of others"*
— Eleanor Roosevelt

Introduction

Let me start by congratulating you on purchasing this book. By doing so you have demonstrated that you are a proactive business owner looking for solutions to the new economic environment we are all having to operate in.

Too many business owners are in VICTIM mode right now; either complaining or blaming everybody or everything for how their business is performing and refusing to look for new ideas or solutions.

The bad news is that if you picked up this book hoping it is going to sort out all your business problems for you right away, just by reading it – then you are going to be very disappointed – it won't!

Knowledge is NOT power as you may have been taught in the past: IMPLEMENTED knowledge is where the real power lies.

The good news is that I have implemented and tested the strategies outlined in this book with hundreds of business owners, (so you are not alone), who have faced serious commercial problems. Some self-inflicted, some the result of circumstances beyond their control such as the current global downturn.

I'm here to tell you that the vast majority have not only survived, but thrived, prospered and profited while others in their industries have panicked or, worse still, perished!

The first thing I want you to grasp firmly is this: it's not the problem, it's what you do about it that counts. In the following pages I have outlined proven battle-tested strategies which are simple, fast to implement and highly effective. If you implement them in your own business, I can tell you now that you will survive and thrive. You'll have more enquires, more sales, better cash flow, increased profit margins, a better performing team and more time to work *on* your business, as opposed to *in* your business, than you've ever dreamed of.

However, I must make it clear right now it's YOU who has to put these strategies into action. I have coached many clients through implementing strategies for change in their business, but it is always *they* who have to actually make the changes. Flicking through the strategies and ideas in this book and just thinking about them is NOT enough – you have to take action.

Actually, though you might not want to hear this right now, I have a feeling that the current recession could result in wonderful things for your future! Many of us have enjoyed running successful businesses over the last few years without too many problems, and in such circumstances it is easy to lose sight of the way a business should be run.   The deadly disease of complacency can sneak into the minds of your sales, accounting, production and management teams, subtle and undetected symptoms going unnoticed or ignored – until it's potentially too late. If you thoroughly overhaul, examine and improve your business systems to survive a severe recession – think how well you'll be doing when it's over – and history tells us that no matter how bad it may be, it WILL pass.

Where you'll be in 12 months from now will be a direct reflection of the new ideas you learn and the strategies you IMPLEMENT in your business.

From my experience of coaching business owners just like you, I know there are enough proven ideas in this book to help your business go from surviving to thriving, whatever industry or market sector you are in. So, now we've covered the basics. There's so much more to cover, I don't want to delay your future success any longer, let's jump right in and get going!

Why Listen to ME?

First let me take just a few words to explain why you should listen to my ideas about moving your business from surviving to thriving – even in the current climate.

Not only have I started, grown, run and sold a number of highly successful businesses myself over the last 17 years, but I also have extensive experience in sales, sales management, marketing, personal development, training and business management. Plus over a 6 year track record as an Award Winning Business Coach.

Paul and Sue Avins

(This award was to recognise the PROFIT growth my clients had achieved and was measured against over 800 coaches from across the world!)

I've had the opportunity to start a business with large amounts of investment and see it grow beyond my wildest expectations, only to lose everything when my investments in many 'Dot.com' businesses turned sour. I've built companies from scratch, having started with less than £100 to my name, and today I run two companies and sit on the Board of several others. I'm operating in the same economy as you are so I know the challenges, I understand the pressures and how to capitalise on the opportunities.

I have also educated and motivated thousands of business owners from across the world through my seminars, workshops and as a keynote speaker. I've consulted with many industries and spoken for some of the largest companies in the world as they battle the new realities.

Outside the VW National Conference after presenting Turbo Marketing

In my commitment to learn even more powerful tools to grow businesses, born out of a desire to save both time and money, I've been mentored by many masters from many fields and, perhaps most importantly of all, I have personally coached hundreds of business owners, in over 79 industries – including coaching a number of my clients to becoming millionaires...

Introduction

The thousands of hours I have spent working with and mentoring business owners over the last 6 years, meant that when the current economic situation began to have an impact on the business community, my strategies and techniques were already battle tested and ready for action. In fact, the strategies you're about to learn have generated millions of pounds of extra profits and sales for my clients and should come with a warning on the cover of this book to say 'VERY HOT, handle with care!'

Paul coaching a business owner

You'll see real client case studies and examples through this book to show just what can be achieved. Here is a great example from a long-term coaching client of mine:

Client Case Study

"Since working with Paul, our business has seen a dramatic and sustained improvement in both revenue and profit. Through his guidance, we've managed to double our turnover every year for the last 3 years. This was achieved through a combination of innovative marketing strategies, close management of costs and an unstinting focus on our business vision. The end result is a company that now not only exceeds our initial dreams but is also more fun and stimulating to run. Paul has been and continues to be a vital element in Eyeful's success."

— Simon Morton (MD), Eyeful Presentations

I decided to write this book both to document what works in the real world right now, so this book is as current as it gets. As well as wanting to give business owners like you access to information that my private business coaching clients pay thousands of pounds for.

I hope you find the answers you are looking for, whatever business you are in and whatever challenge you are facing.

Here's to your future success!

How to Use This Book

When writing this book I wanted to use my own extensive experience as well as the many brilliant ideas and strategies generated by clients and mentors over many years. This book can be used in one of two ways.

Because the book is divided into chapters covering the key business sections, each strategy can stand alone. You can implement the strategies in the order that works best for you depending on YOUR business and its needs.

- **Firstly : You can use it as if you are going to the supermarket**, you buy what you need for that day or week and come back again and again as you need different food and drink at different times.

You will notice that some of the strategies appear in more than one chapter. This occurs for a number of reasons, but mainly I wanted to ensure that whatever section you chose to delve into, the answer would be waiting there for you. Also, the adage that repetition is the mother of learning is true. "To know and not to do, is not to know". So if you find yourself thinking, hold on – I've read this before... take a moment to consider why you haven't implemented it yet!

If you read a strategy and think – "Yes, I could do that" – then stop reading and GO DO IT!

The book will still be here when you've implemented the strategy and started to generate new sales and profits.

- **Secondly: You can read this book straight through,** so you get a full view of all the strategies and how they fit and work together. Then you can work through to the 90-day action plan to lay out your recession-beating blueprint.

The book is designed to be read, worked through and referred to, depending on the time you have and your motivation level.

I've put in questions to stimulate and challenge you, as a good coach would, as well as including key ideas, learning points and action plans at the end of some of the chapters.

Below are three icons I've placed throughout the book to make certain points more memorable.

- *Question Mark* where I have placed important questions.

- *Key* where there are key ideas for you to pay extra attention to and to refer to for speed.

- *Exclamation Mark* for items I want you to pay attention to because they could be just what your business needs right now.

If you have any questions you can ask me directly by visiting **www.AskPaulAvins.com** and I'll answer as many as I can on my Blogs.

One thing I have learned reading hundreds of books relating to business, leadership, spirituality, success and motivation is that you'll absorb more if you have a clear goal of what you want to learn from the material. It gives your brain a focus and a target to seek out.

So... stop for a moment and think of the top 3 outcomes you want from reading this book:

1 ....

....

....

2. ....

....

....

3. ....

....

....

Chapter 1:

Facing A New World Reality

> *"The ones who are crazy enough to think they can change the world, are the ones who do!"*
>
> — Steve Jobs (Founder of Apple Inc.)

A Shock to the System

There is no getting away from the fact that since September 2008 from September 2008 the world went into a financial meltdown triggered, as we all now know, by the banks buying billions of pounds worth of toxic assets.

This was the trigger that shot down the global economic boom that many had thought would see the end of the boom-and-bust cycle forever. In fact, many politicians even said so publicly. With so many people buying into this new vision of "easy money and profits" emotionally, when the crash came it shook people's belief systems to the core. Businesses that had seemed invincible and at the heart of our way of life disappeared in just months. Woolworths, MFI and Cobra Beer to name three Even major institutions like the banks and insurance companies had to be saved from collapse by tax payers and governments all around the world.

The ripples of these events are now starting to be felt in all markets. Some of the ripples bring opportunity, other ripples bring pain. The latest figures from top insolvency specialists Begbies Traynor say that over 40,000 small or medium businesses in the UK will go bust in the next 12 months, further adding to the unemployment numbers which are rapidly heading for 3 million in the UK alone. This figure will be 18% higher than at the peak of the 1990 recession.

When a shock occurs some people freeze up and see just red stop lights everywhere, while others assess the situation and look for the way forward.

Wherever there is great uncertainty there is usually great opportunity, if you know how to see it, and then how to exploit it. This book is designed to give you the tools to do both.

If you have been caught at an emotional red light, STOP blaming yourself. When you use language like "I should have done this or I could have done that...." all it does is focus you on the past – and there is no business there. We all have 20/20 hindsight, but the reality is that nobody predicted the speed of this recession, so shake off any sense of guilt or blame and get ready to start profiting while others are panicking.

The Only Constant IS Change

A question I am consistently asked by business owners all over the world who hear me speak at my seminars or as a guest at others' events:

"How can I possibly succeed in the current recession as my margins are being squeezed and demand is down?"

It's a fair question and I know how they feel. After all, I have had many clients since September '08 experience the same problem. What I found is that the clients who are willing and open to change, change their products, change their service, change their pricing structures, even change their banks, are finding new markets, coming up with new ideas and new value propositions that are moving them towards the success they desire.

The challenge is that most business owners want to have a different outcome without having to change what they are currently doing.

OK, time for a reality check:

CHANGE IS THE ONLY CONSTANT!

Anything else is just an illusion. Change brings Opportunity and Opportunity brings Wealth. Just look what happens when new technology enters a market or a change in government legislation  occurs. New businesses spring up to take advantage and wealth is created. Before the creation of eBay in 1995, who would have thought that millions of people could sell their unwanted junk for a profit to a worldwide market from their own bedrooms?

The first mobile phone call in the UK was only made in 1985, but that industry has already created a number of millionaires and even billionaires. And it was the de-regulation of franchise laws in the US that lead to Ray Crock taking the blue print of a successful local restaurant and turning it into the global phenomenon that is McDonalds.

It's a universal law that we are either growing or dying, there is no standing still, and in the current climate change is happening faster than ever, so you better be on the road to change or you run the risk of being one of the next 100,000 businesses to perish!

Sometimes the death of something, a business, an industry or an economy has to happen before the re-birth or a new birth can take place. We are heading into a new economic time and it's natural for old business models to die out, so don't be alarmed by this. Do be alarmed if your business is running one of these old models!

The Birth of a New Economy

Ask any parent, including me, about the birth of their first child. Usually it was a long-drawn-out process involving a lot of hard work, considerable pain at times and huge amounts of emotional worry but in the end it was all SO worth it.

The same is true for the global economy right now. What you are experiencing is the first few hours of labour. When it's all over we will all be left with a new world and a new economic reality, which is why expecting things to go back to the way they were before is just NEVER going to happen.

The largest shifting demographic in history is happening right now with the 'baby boomer' generation about to start hitting retirement in the next few years. This WILL drive massive change as people in their 60s and 70s have very different spending habits, with very different disposable incomes. Add to this the fact that the life cycle of a business has been speeded up by new technology. What used to take 5-10 years to work through in total can now happen in just 3-5 years, and, in some markets, such as on-line, it can be even faster than that!

The Business Cycle has been Speeded up – Forever

Innovation or *Start up* to *Rapid Expansion* to *Market Maturity* to *Market Saturation* to *Decline* and *Destruction*, then back to *Innovation*.

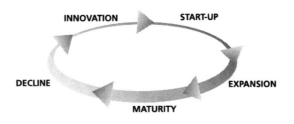

As well as adding speed into the business mix, almost like a spark in a fuel injector, technology has put power in the hands of your customers like never before. Over 85% of people now research a purchase on-line before buying it.

Internet shopping is predicted to hit $145.1 billion in the coming year says Google, a significant 14% increase – despite the recession!

Today's customers are more educated, know more about your competition and how good your prices are, than ever before. Add to this the fact that, through Social Networks, bad customer service is broadcast to thousands in just minutes and you'll see that, if you're not in tune with these shifts, you'll be out of the market in record time.

The web has been at the heart of the Information Age, but people are now overwhelmed with information so what they want is distilled advice they can trust. We are at the start of the Referral Age™ and what business owners hunger for most these days is trusted advisors. More on this in the Sales section of the book (page 79).

When you are looking at what is happening from this positive point of view, I am willing to bet you get excited about where you and your business could be 3 to 5 years from now.

But there is a warning that could kill your new-found energy...

The Killer Number in Your Business

When I do Strategic Planning with my clients we look at lots of different areas of the business. We conduct a SWOT analysis, (assessing Strengths, Weaknesses, Opportunities and Threats), and look for the future hot markets in their sectors. There is a critical question that I find identifies where the potential problems of the future may spring from and it's this:

"Where in your business does the number '1' occur?"

Let me explain...

When you have 1 of anything you could find yourself with problems. Here are just some of the areas you may want to review:

- 1 Major Customer generating large profits for you

- 1 Major Supplier that you rely on for the majority of your sales

- 1 Bank Account / Finance source

- 1 Lead Source or Marketing Method

- 1 Key team member who knows how to perform a critical function

- 1 Top Sales Person who brings in all your business

- 1 Referral System

- 1 Product that is responsible for all of your Profit

- 1 Route to market or 1 way to purchase from you

If one of these fails in your business – You're out of Business, Game Over!

Take a moment to list the top 3 areas in your business where the number 1 makes an appearance and then start to eliminate this dependency on just 1.

1 ....

....

....

2. ....

....

....

3. ....

....

....

If you have any questions on this chapter...

Go to **www.AskPaulAvins.com** and ask me!

"A ship in harbor is safe – but that
is not what ships are built for"

— John A. Shedd

Chapter 2:

Building your Entrepreneur Mindset

> *"The definition of insanity is doing the same thing over and over and expect different results!"*
>
> — Albert Einstein

Adopt a Start-Up Mentality

During a recent coaching session, I asked one of my clients which single strategy did she feel was having the biggest positive impact in moving her business forward in the current economic climate?

She thought for a moment then said that going back and acting like she had when she first started her business all those years ago had been the best thing she had done.

Think about that for a moment. The idea that no matter how big or successful (or not, for that matter!) your business is right now, the adoption of this start-up attitude of speed, flexibility, hunger, a passion for innovation and an openness to learning, all combined, could just be the edge you've been looking for.

So how do you develop this mindset?

Here are my top ideas for you to implement:

Develop Greater Mental Toughness

The World's leading expert on Mental Toughness – Steve Siebold says:

> *"Amateur performers operate from delusion, pros operate from objective reality. The great ones' habits, actions and behaviours are totally congruent with the size and scope of their ultimate vision. That's why we call them champions!"*
>
> www.speakerstevesiebold.com

Re-visit your Vision for your business and your life. Is it big enough to give you the energy and power to grow stronger through this global adversity? If not, what do you need to do to magnify your Vision until it is that powerful for you?

Decide to Survive – then Thrive

Now DECIDE to achieve your Vision. There is great power built into the decision-making process. Have you ever found that the hardest part of decision-making is deciding whether you need to make a decision in the first place? But once you have decided, actually achieving your goal seems to take a lot less effort than you had anticipated. Events conspire to help you in ways you had never imagined. People and resources seem to magically appear just when you need them most.

So, what stops most people from charging ahead into the success they desire? It's one thing... FEAR. Fear is often referred to as False Emotions Appearing Real and it's never been more true than in today's world with the emotional levels at an all-time high, and sensationalist scaremongering being reported as fact in the press.

Courage is Acting in Spite of Fear

> *"Do the thing you fear and the death of fear is certain."*
>
> —Ralph Waldo Emerson

In my experience of working with some of the most successful people in their industries, this critical skill sees them through, no matter what obstacle they are facing.

The funny thing is that people who fail seem to think successful people don't have any fears or doubts – this is just not the case. They do, but successful people have conditioned themselves to take the appropriate action even if inside they are shaking and fearful.

The business owners who face their fears and act anyway will thrive during this recession. Others, who let fear stop them taking action, will ultimately see the result in lost sales, lost profits and, potentially, a lost business.

I remember being at one of my first Tony Robbins seminar, (if you have not been to one I strongly recommend you go), and after hearing him tell his story he shared a powerful affirmation that has stuck with me ever since... If I can't – then I MUST!

Next time you find yourself facing fear in your business or your personal life, simply repeat this affirmation 10 times out loud until you feel the energy of action flow through your body – then act!

2 – Building Your Entrepreneur Mindset

Feed Yourself Positive Mind Food

"You can never earn in the outside world more than you earn in your own mind."

— Brian Tracy, Author and Speaker

www.briantracy.com

One of the oldest laws in the Universe is that we become what we think about. And, in my experience, the best way to control what you think about is to commit to feeding your mind positive, uplifting and educating information on a daily basis.

What you put in your mind first thing sets your focus for the rest of the day, so set yourself up to win with 30 minutes of positive reading, meditation or listening to personal development CDs every morning.

At the other end of the day, while your conscious mind sleeps, you want your subconscious mind working for you, so read something stimulating or spend time visualising. What I mean by this is that for the last 30 minutes of every day you should try to create a mental image of the perfect outcome or solution that you desire.

Please don't just take my word for this – test it for yourself for 21 days and see just how much better you feel and how much more you achieve.

After all, if you want to change something in your life, you have to change some things in your life!

With so much negative news around us, we need to build our own self-supporting habits.

Energy Flows Where Attention Goes

> *"Whether it's a positive or negative vibration, the Law of Attraction will give you more of the same"*
>
> — Michael Losier, Law of Attraction Coach and Author
>
> www.lawofattractionbook.com

Whatever you focus on you will get more of – that's the Universal Law of Attraction, and you can argue with me all you like but I've seen it manifest in my own life again and again, as well as in the lives of my clients.

I have one client who is always telling me what he doesn't want to happen in his business, and how bad it would be if it did! He is giving this unwanted outcome so much attention it's hardly surprising when he creates the very thing he fears!

I know that when everything looks bleak it can be hard to focus on what you want. When I got myself into over £80,000 of credit card debt and had a hard time just covering the interest payments, every fibre of my being wanted to focus on all the bad stuff happening.

But, as one of my coaches said to me, "Anybody can do this when things are going well, that's easy. The real question is, can you do it when it's hard or do you just give up, go home and wish it was easier?"

You WILL get more of what you focus on – FACT. So choose to focus on all the good things you want to happen in your business and life – new clients or contracts you want to win, the profits you want to make and the amazing team you want to build.

What are the top 3 things you want more of in your life
right now?

1 ....

....

....

2. ....

....

....

3. ....

....

....

Look for the Silver Linings

In the great personal development classic, Think and Grow Rich,
Napoleon Hill, who studied successful people for over 25 years,
discovered something amazing.

Even very successful people, (including J.D. Rockefeller –
who made his fortune in the great depression of the 1930's) had
a certain habit.

Napoleon Hill described it as: "Looking for the seed of equal or greater benefit in every adversity".

You probably know it better as "every cloud has a silver lining". Think back to your own business or life. Think about the times when you have had an unexpected adversity hit a project or sale you were working on. What better outcome did you end up achieving because the adversity forced you to think differently or to change your approach?

Lock in this learning by capturing it below:

....

....

....

From now on when adversity shows up – welcome it as the major opportunity it disguises. Your job is to see beyond the disguise, recognize the opportunity and act!

You Win or You Learn

A great belief to develop is that you win or you learn – there is no such thing as failure.

Failure occurs if you give up forever and stop moving forward. Motivational Speaker Les Brown says: "When life knocks you down, be sure to land on your back because if you can look up you can get up!"

There is no such thing as failure in business, there is just feedback designed to help you get better next time. You may not like some of the feedback to date, that's OK. Just decide to learn from it and move forward to your next success.

Break Even or Bust?

> *"Business IS Simple but that does not mean it's easy!"*
>
> — Paul Avins

You have to fight for your right to Profit! Nobody is going to hand it to you on a plate, nor should they.

It's key to your success that you know and monitor your break-even costs at all times. Think back to start-up days when you only spent what you absolutely HAD to, and you re-used what you could and begged or borrowed in order to keep costs down.

A £1 saved can be as good as £5 sold when you take all the costs into account, so while I agree that you can't cost-cut your way to success in this climate, you can manage your costs as aggressively as possible.

More on this in the *Profit Margins* section, page 123.

Chase Every Potential Sale

Remember how, in the early days of starting your business, you chased and hustled hard? If there was even a slight chance that somebody would buy from you, you followed up relentlessly until they said emphatically "No".

The challenge is that as a business grows, what I call Follow-Up Fatigue™ creeps in and sales opportunities start to slip through your fingers. In today's world, these lost sales can be the difference between success and failure.

I'll cover how to implement a powerful marketing follow-up system in the Marketing chapter, but for now I want you to commit to adopt the mind set of "They buy or they die!" – and these are the only two ways they get out o f your follow-up system!

This does not mean you apply pressure-selling techniques – far from it in fact, but what it does mean is that you focus on your follow up. A buyer is a buyer is a buyer, and if they raised their hand out of interest they are in the market for your product or service. If not now then at some point in the future. You just need to be ready when they are ready to order.

Client Case Study

"In the last 12 months, Paul's Coaching has really helped me to think bigger about my business. My profits are now up over 200% on last year and we are still growing - you can't argue with results like that!"

— Jill Treloggen (MD), Jill Treloggen Interiors
www.jilltreloggeninteriors.com

Add MASSIVE Value

Life, and indeed business rewards you in direct proportion to the amount of value you add to other people.

The interesting part is that often the rewards do not come directly from the person you've added the value to. This concept took me a long time to figure out!

When you finally understand this – it becomes far easier to be a Go-Giver than a Go-Getter, which should enable you to constantly answer the question, "How can I add more value to my prospects, my customers and my team?"

It's important that you consistently strive to add massive value and that this concept is a core value in your business.

Collect your Cash – Fast

When your business is in start-up mode you need every penny you can get as fast as you can get it, because you usually don't have access to huge lines of bank credit or finance.

In today's world this is more true than ever.
Yes, the Governments are trying to force the banks to lend again, but the reality is, it's your responsibility to get the cash you are owed as fast as possible.

In the cash flow section of this book I offer many, easy-to-implement strategies to make this happen. If this is an area of pain for your business you may want to go straight to that chapter first on page 105.

Opportunity is ...?

Try this quick test – Look at the following words and letters –

Opportunity is **NOWHERE**

What do you see?

Is Opportunity **NO WHERE**

or......

Is Opportunity **NOW HERE?**

Same letters, very different results and emotions!

The worst thing any business can do right now is to adopt a wait-and-see attitude and decide to do nothing at all!

With the right mind-set backed by solid strategies to help you, you can and will move your business forward despite the negative press surrounding us right now.

Here are a few examples of companies who started up or grew rapidly during recessions and depressions:

- GE (General Electric) – Started in the recession of 1873 by inventor Thomas Edison, now the third largest company in the world.

- HP (Hewlett-Packard) – Started at the end of the Great Depression. First technology business to achieve sales of over $100 billion.

- Burger King – Started in the 1954 recession, today in over 65 countries.

- Microsoft – The 1975 recession saw Bill Gates launch Microsoft and the rest, as they say, is history.

- Amazon.com – The start of 1998 saw the launch of Amazon.com, now a Fortune 500 company with revenues in the Billions… and growing.

- BBC2 Dragon James Cann started his Global Recruitment business Alexander Mann during the 1980s Recession.

The key, as always, is to look for a gap in the market, or to see an opportunity to refine a business model in order to deliver what customers want, faster, more efficiently or to a larger market place than before.

I predict that out of this current recession new and globally positioned businesses will be birthed and will grow.

The question I have is – will your business be one of these success stories?

Get the REAL Picture

Before you can even start to look at ways to improve your business right now you need to get a reality check and see what's really happening in order to set a base line from which you can move forward. And trust me, I'm going to give you a lot of strategies and tools you can use which will improve your business.

After all, if you don't know where you are, how can you possibly start to plan your way to a future of greater sales, profits and success?

During the thousands of hours I've spent coaching my clients over the years, it is always the clarity of these questions that seems to unlock the door to a brighter future for them.

Here are some KEY Power Questions to ask yourself before we go any further:

- What's really happening in my business right now? Be 100% honest with yourself!

....

....

....

- What's really happening in my industry right now? Is it growing or dying?

....

....

....

- What is the No.1 problem facing my customers right now that, if I could solve for them, would have them breaking down my door? If you don't know – ASK!

....

....

....

- What is my current cash position?

....

....

- What is the sales trend for the last 6 months?

....

....

....

- What is the sales pipeline like for the next 90 days?

....

....

- What is the biggest drag or drain (product, service, location etc) on my business and how can I cut it free?

....

....

....

- Where is the biggest opportunity for growth in my business in the next 12 months?

....

....

....

- What is my personal level of belief in my business to succeed in the current climate? 1-10, 10 being very high!

....

....

Chapter 3:

Marketing

> *"A business has but two functions –*
> *Marketing and Innovation."*
>
> — Tom Peters, Management Guru

The Power of Response-Driven Marketing

I believe that becoming a great response-driven marketer is one of the most important skills that an entrepreneur or business owner can master. After all, as the great copywriter Gary Halbert once said, *"There is no business problem that can't be solved by a great sales letter."*

The skill is to get prospects and customers to raise their hands and say, "I want to buy more from you!" If you can do this in these tough economic times, your business will thrive on a level higher than you've ever imagined up to now.

In this section, you'll find a mix of fundamental marketing concepts and ideas that you'll need to master, along with easy-to-implement techniques my coaching clients are using right now to grow their businesses.

The only area not covered here is Internet Marketing as I feel this is so important that I have given it its own chapter.

OK... let's get stuck into the strategies. Make sure you have a highlighter handy to select the ones you want to implement right away.

Invest more Cash into Marketing

Now this may seem very odd considering that your business may be cash-strapped right now but the reality is that 90% of businesses will cut back on marketing, which leaves a great opportunity for you.

In the last recession, McDonalds tripled their advertising budget and took huge market share from their biggest competitor, Burger King. You can do the same in your market if you implement some of the ideas listed on these pages.

Remember: if done correctly, your marketing should always deliver a return far greater than your investment in it, which means you can outgun your competition and make more sales.

Test and Measure Everything and Stop What's Not Working

Many business owners conduct marketing as if they were playing darts in the dark. They know there is a bull's eye (customer) out there somewhere, but they have no real idea where until they get lucky. Even then, because they have no feedback mechanism, hitting the bull's eye again is almost impossible.

So... let's dispel an old myth – "50% of my marketing works – I just don't know which 50%!". Yes, I know it's a joke – but sadly it has been a reality in many of the businesses I have looked at over the years, and settling for this way of thinking has businesses wasting hundreds of thousands of pounds on strategies that don't even cover their costs.

The answer?

Test, measure and track how every one of your marketing strategies is performing. Start with just asking new prospects how they heard about you and write down the results (this in itself is an innovation for many). Then, at the end of the month, look at which strategies didn't generate any enquiries, or very few, and which didn't convert into orders, and simply stop them.

Key Idea: You must test and measure your existing marketing strategy's performance before you start making changes to it – otherwise you could destroy something that is working well for you already.

Know Your Marketing KPIs (Key Performance Indicators)

Most people think marketing is all about creativity, whereas in reality it's more about maths and process than just "blue sky thinking..."

To be able to judge if a marketing initiative is working for you, you will need to track the following Key Performance Indicators,

- how many leads did the campaign bring to the business?

- how many of these leads converted into sales?

- what was the average order value of each sale?

- how many times did those customers repeat buy from you?

- what margin were those sales made at?

Give each campaign you run a unique reference number (whether it be on direct mail, email, magazine/press adverts or telemarketing campaigns) for customers to use when contacting or ordering from you. Once you are armed with this information it is very easy to see at a glance which campaigns are worth running again and which aren't.

Spend Time getting to the Heart of Your Target Market

Before conducting any marketing or advertising you need to know EXACTLY WHO you are wanting to talk to. It's not enough to be general and say men aged 20-35 or women with 2 children. You need to get very, very specific or your market will not respond to your message.

Key Idea: You are marketing to one person at a time. Even if you are using a mass advertising medium such as a magazine advert, there is only one person reading it at a time. Your message has to talk their language and convey the feelings the reader or viewer relates and connects to.

You also need to become comfortable with the fact that it is OK to de-select people and to project yourself into a "micro niche". Customers will pay more for products and services that are clearly designed just for their specific situation rather than for mass-market we-want-to-be-everything-to-everybody solutions.

The better you know and understand your customers, the more connection you can have with your target market, through better marketing copy and images that they will relate to.

Here are some questions to consider:

- What age is your ideal client? ....

- Are they male or female? ....

- Where do they live? Town, city, county, country?

  ....

- Do they have children? If so, how many? Boys or girls? What age?

  ....

- What newspapers or magazines do they like to read?

  ....

  ....

- What do they do for a living?

  ....

- What type of car do they drive?

  ....

- What are their passions and hobbies?

  ....

  ....

  ....

- What is currently worrying them and keeping them awake at night?

....

....

....

- What is their biggest emotional fear about buying what you offer?

....

....

....

- Do they prefer to shop on-line for your product or services?

....

- How much do they earn?

....

Client Case Study

"Following Paul's advice we have maintained a positive attitude, increased our marketing activity and implemented many of his recession beating strategies. Enquiries were up over 100% year on year in January 09 with a conversion rate of 60%. February enquiries are up 30% with an 85% conversion rate so far."

— Niall Douglas, Full Circle Travel
www.fullcircletravel.com

Revisit your USP (Unique Selling Point) and Make it Stronger

Never, ever be a "me too" type of a business if you want to succeed in the short or long term. The market, and by that we mean customers, hate businesses that are not unique.

If you are not unique then, be warned, you could soon be extinct!

If you are not sure what is unique about your business, go back and ask your customers? Find out why they buy from you... you'll often be surprised, because it is not always the obvious things that you've been focusing on to date.

Now if you are saying... "Our Service" or "Our Prices" or "Quality", then you need to think again because these are what everybody, including your competition, says, and nothing kills a response in marketing like generalities. Nobody hears or believes them any more.

Get specific, right down into the detail – what is it about your service that makes you unique? The speed of delivery? How well qualified your people are? Is it the way you install something?

One last thing to consider when defining your USP, if a customer can say, "Well I should hope you do" to it – it's nowhere close to a Unique Selling Point. The key word of those three is Selling, and your uniqueness must compel people to buy from you over your competition.

Put a Strong Guarantee in Place

As I travel and speak to business audiences across the world I ask them this question:

"How many of you currently have a strong, clear guarantee that you use in all your marketing?" On average less than 10% of the room will put their hands up. Then I ask...

"How many of you, if you had an unhappy customer, would do whatever it took to sort out the problems to keep them happy?" Now everyone's hand is up!

My point is this: if you would do all this if somebody complained then you already have a guarantee – YOU ARE JUST NOT TELLING PEOPLE about it and it could be costing you thousands of pounds in lost sales.

Go back, look at what you would do and see how you can turn it into a guarantee that will give people the confidence to buy from you.

Paul's Guarantee

If you don't re-coup your investment in this book and make a return of x10 using these strategies 60 days after you purchased it, send it back for a no questions asked, no hard feelings, refund!

Take a moment to answer these questions:

- What is the one thing that really frustrates your customers about dealing with your industry?

....

....

....

....

- What is the one thing *you could guarantee* that, if you told your customers about it, would have them running for their credit cards to place an order?

....

....

....

....

Now all you have to do is figure out HOW you are going to deliver a guarantee that addresses this and you'll have more sales than you know what to do with.

Warning: Make sure you have tested this on a small scale first to be certain you can manage the increase in business when you roll it out on a large scale.

Client Story

I once coached an artist who was having difficulties closing sales for the large pieces of her art at over £5,000 price point. People loved them but never bought them. I suggested she implemented a try it FREE in your home for 30 day approach which guaranteed no charge while you see if you liked living with it. At the end of the first month she made two sales.

Use a Powerful P.S. at the End of your Sales Letters

Far too many businesses send letters to introduce a product or service, essentially a sales letter and then end the letter without a P.S. of any kind. This is crazy as some people will just read the key points of the letter and the P.S. is one of these.

Postscripts (the PS at the end of the letter) can increase your sales by as much as 30%! How amazing is that?!!? Jay Abraham, one of the world's top Marketers and a mentor and trainer of mine, has tested this strategy again and again with his clients.

When he's added a powerful P.S. to an already profitable sales letter, the response rates have increased by up to 30%. If it worked for him it will work for you as long as it's got a strong benefit in it for the reader – and a call to action.

Look at What Used to Work but which You've Now Stopped Doing

I once had a full-page advert to promote my Business Coaching Practice in the early days of starting my business. After a couple of tests, I hit on a formula that generated appointments and clients and was, over a 12-month period, very profitable.

Then I got busy and stopped running it because I became bored with it! How dumb was that? Yet many businesses I coach have done exactly the same.

Think about the strategies you have used in the past that delivered you results which for some reason or other you have just stopped using. Could be direct mail, telemarketing, classified adverts – doesn't matter, but go back and start using them again to see if they will still work for you.

So, check you are using your proven strategies first it's cheaper and quicker than starting to test new strategies.

What old strategies do you need to start using again? List them below:

....

....

....

....

....

....

....

....

....

....

Move the FREE Access Point for your Prospects

Some marketers refer to this as "reducing the barrier to entry for your customers", but if FREE is the most powerful word in marketing it makes sense to use it here.

OK... why do I want you to think about giving things away for free?

Well... here are a number of reasons that work:

- It can help you build up your database very quickly, creating a willing audience that you can go back and sell to again and again.

- It builds massive trust with your prospects.

- It WILL increase your conversion rate = more sales.

- It will give your marketing a strong 'Call to Action' (more on this later).

- It will create a BUZZ in your community or market.

- It can help you take market share from your competitors.

Take a moment and think about what you could offer "for free" to get your prospects visiting your web site, shop or calling your sales team.

Here are just a few examples some of my clients have used:

- Free Seminars

- Free Reports / how to save money on <your product> etc

- Free Product Samples

- Free Chapters of a new book / ebook

- Free quotation / valuation

- Free home visit / inspection

- Free finance audit

- Free design (this one was huge in terms of increasing response)

Use Powerful, Customer Benefit-Orientated Headlines

So much marketing fails to use this simple but very powerful strategy. Think about it – if newspapers feel it's critical to get an attention-grabbing headline to motivate you to buy their newspaper or to read an article, the same principle will apply to your own marketing.

When designing your advert, sales letter or the landing page on your web site, you should spend far longer on the headline than you do on the copy. After all, if the headline is weak your prospect will never make it to the copy.

Here are my top headline tips:

- Make it at least 25% of your advert

- Put your killer offer in the headline if you have one

- Make it attention grabbing – use controversy if appropriate

- Have it appear newsworthy – use words like "Announcing"

- Promise a specific benefit to the reader – "Here's how you can ..."

- Put the word YOU in to build rapport ...

- Use a quote from a happy customer ...

Use One-time Offers to Increase your Average Order Value

This approach has been used on-line by Internet marketers for years to great effect. The reality is that any business can offer a new or existing customer a one-time special offer so compelling that a high percentage of prospects or customers will take it.

This is a great profit strategy as well, because you can bundle products or services together to create a higher perceived value and boost your margins!

A word of warning! You must stay true to your word and only offer this once, or your customers will become very sceptical of your future promotions. It also needs a expiry time or date to build a sense of urgency and scarcity so people feel they need to take advantage of it before it expires.

Ask yourself – what could you put in a "WOW" one-time offer?

My WOW offer is:

....

....

....

....

....

....

....

Have a Powerful Call To Action (CTA) in your Marketing

Humans are funny. If you don't tell them exactly what to do to purchase your product or service then in most cases they do nothing and move on to the next page in a magazine or website. You must make it as easy as possible for them to deal with you.

Before running any advertising be clear exactly what your Call To Action will be – what do you want the reader or listener to do and when?

Here are just a few alternatives to be considered:

- Call your sales team

- Book an appointment

- Visit your website or Blog

- Request an information pack

- Place an order

- Subscribe to a newsletter

- Enter a competition

- Test drive a product or service for free

- Introduce a friend

- Follow you on Twitter

My next Call To Action will be:

....

....

....

....

....

....

....

....

....

Clean up and Grow your Database

Today's environment is an ideal time to clean up your database. This should really be done at least every 6-months as it will save you money on wasted deliveries of direct mail and e-mail.

It will also make you money as the cleaner and more detailed the information you hold on your customers, the more personal and relevant the marketing messages you can send them, which will bring you a greater response and more sales.

Note: If you hold any data on your customers, even if it's just their name and address, be sure you are registered with the Data Protection Agency.

http://www.ico.gov.uk/

If you have not been collecting your customers' details, start today as they will hold the key to future profits. Think about all the ways you can ask for their details, but the best time is at time of purchase or with a free large prize draw which increases their willingness to give you their information.

Build a 12-month Marketing Calendar

So many businesses waste thousands of pounds a year on impulse marketing that never delivers results, yet by taking a few hours to plan, this could all be eliminated.

In my experience, impulse purchases of advertising rarely deliver good results, as the space left is usually in the wrong place on the page or right at the back of the publication.

Take time to plan your marketing. Look at each month and see how you can use events like Valentine's Day, Easter, Hanukah, Eid or Christmas to theme your message and make it topical.

Run a marketing calendar for two years, testing and measuring as you go, and you'll develop a powerful, proven system which will serve you for a long time.

Leverage your Time and Resources

This is all about working smarter, not harder. If you are already doing some marketing or have assets such as logoed vehicles or business cards, make sure they are working for you as hard as they can be from a marketing point of view.

- Have an offer on the back of your business card

- Send out offers in all regular mail such as statements or invoices

- Put a board up outside your premises to attract passing customers

- Drop flyers into offices or homes around where you may already be working, (this alone generated £100,000 of new business for a client of mine, and only cost £200 for the printing and some time delivering them)

- Have strong CTAs on company vans, etc. The AA are great at this as they actually have a sign saying, "Join today, ask the driver" (who is probably on a commission as well!).

Implement a Regular Communication System

How many times have we all heard a customer say to us, "I didn't know you did that!" when we point out that what they just bought from our competition they could have bought from us.

This is a CRIME for us as business owners and we should do everything in our power to make sure it never happens again.

So... today, COMMIT to implementing a system of a regular education-based marketing plan. Start sending out newsletters that cross-promote the products and services you sell. If you don't want to do it yourself, outsource it to a copywriter – it will pay for itself many times over.

The key to results from a newsletter is consistent communication. After all, how many of us have seen companies proudly announce their first newsletter – never to be seen or heard from again?

Client Case Study

A client of mine had a database that was 11 years of past customer data that, when I started working with him, he had never marketed to! We started running physical paper newsletters every 4 months and 4 years later we are still doing it. The result is that every time we run them he gets a boost in business. **In 4 years his sales are up over 500% and still growing!**

Nobody said this was always going to be easy. Yes, it takes hard work, but if you are serious about success, what did you expect?

Create a Customer of the Month Award!

For marketing to work and work well it needs to have a number of elements, but the most overlooked is FUN!

This strategy is very simple, but it doesn't mean that you should underestimate its power to deliver you extra business and content for your newsletter.

Every month, randomly select a customer of the month. Have something fun delivered to their offices or home as a prize and ensure you take a picture handing it over. This provides proof for your sceptical prospects and customers and an ethical bribe to the winning company or person to keep using your service.

Soon everybody who places an order with you will be subconsciously thinking, "Will I be the next customer of the month?"
And guess what? Some people will order more so that they have more chances of winning!

Collect and Publish more Testimonials

No matter how big a business you are or how long
you've been trading, new customers are worried
before they place their order. In fact, even your
existing customers will have concerns before they
try new products or services. They'll be asking:

• Will you do what it says in your brochure or on your website?

• Can I trust you?

• If I pay on-line will I actually get what I ordered?

• What happens if I am not happy with what I bought?

The list goes on and on. The best way to address this is through the
strategic use of customers' testimonials.

• Hang them framed in your reception.

• Send them out with every quote you do. If you can match the
  industry types or geographic locations to your prospects it will
  increase response rates.

• Put them in your adverts, newsletters, mail shots.

• Put them on your website and in video format if you can – it doesn't
  need to be expensive – buy a Flip Camera from Amazon and be sure
  to record any happy customer you come into contact with.

• Make sure you use the customer's full name and location,
  and provide their photo if possible to prove they are real, as people
  are sceptical.

You can never have enough testimonials, so set goals to collect them
and set up a system to ask new customers for them after 90 days.

Build a Customer Loyalty Program to Lock in Future Profits

I have a shocking truth for you!

Customer Satisfaction is a waste of time!

Now, I know you may disagree with me, but let me explain. How many times have you been to a restaurant and had average food that you were *satisfied* with. You even told the waiter it was good when he asked so as not to offend him.

But... (and this is the key question) did you ever go back? Perhaps once more just to see if it had improved?

The reality is that the only currency that matters is customer loyalty. You need to do WHATEVER it takes to keep them loyal because now more than ever the battle for every pound in their pocket is intense, so if you deliver anything less than exceptional service they'll be gone for good.

Create a loyalty programme where frequent buyers (members) get added bonuses not available to non-members. Have branded cards printed and ask everybody who buys from you if they want to join. After all it's as if you are giving them FREE MONEY, yet in reality you are saving yourself thousands of pounds that you would be having to spend to generate new customers if they left you for your competition.

Note: make sure the benefits you give have a high perceived cost and a low actual cost so that you maintain as much of your margin as possible.

Learn how to Write more Emotional, Rapport-Building Copy

In sales, people buy on emotion 80% of the time and back up their decision with logic the other 20%.

Claude Hopkins, the great advertising legend, used to say that, "Advertising is just Salesmanship in Print". I believe this is true for all marketing media today. So if it's going to sell me on your product or service you have to get a lot of emotion into your copy.

Client stories are a great way to do this as they have the human element of drama already built in.

Study copy writing and record sales meetings with customers. Transcribe the conversations looking for key words or phrases you or they used that you could use in marketing material.

Become Aware of the I Versus You Ratio

When so many business owners write an advert, newsletter or sales letter, they fall into the trap of talking about what is, to them, the most interesting subject in their world – THEMSELVES!

The following technique keeps you focused on your customer and ensures your ego stays in check. Here's how it works...

When you have written your advert, letter, website, etc., go back and count the number of times you use the words: I, We, Our, Us or your Company Name. Then count the number of times you use:
You or Your. Work out the ratio and see where your focus is – is it on your customer or on you?

Your goal is to have a 3:1 ratio in favour of your customer.
This makes them feel more important and that you are talking to them personally – both of which will increase your sales.

Higher Frequency = Higher Results

Your goal as a business owner should be to always be in the mind of your prospect or customer so that whenever they think of your product or service they think of you and do business with you.

Most people subscribe to the stop-start-stop approach to marketing which seldom delivers strong or lasting results.

You must get your message in front of your prospects or customers on a regular basis, daily, weekly or monthly at the longest.

The more often you talk to them with relevant messages (the key here is to educate and not always sell, sell, sell), the faster you become their trusted adviser in your field. And people do business with people they trust – FACT!

Start Using very Targeted Direct Mail

The great opportunity today is very targeted, personalised direct mail.

With everybody trying to cut costs by using e-mail, the fact is there is less competition in your prospect's letter box so your message is more likely to get read and acted on.

You can buy very targeted lists of prospects now for just about anything and everything, whatever your market, whether B2C or B2B (business to consumer or business to business), and you can even send your message to Managing Directors' home addresses if you wish.

Remember: the more targeted your message, the higher your response rate will be. Relevance = Response.

Personalise for Profit

We are all exposed to so many messages a day that if we don't feel a message is specifically for us we ignore it.

The great news is that with Digital Print and On-line technology you can now send very targeted, highly personalised marketing messages to your customers or prospects from your database. This is why collecting information from your prospects and customers is so critical, as I mentioned earlier.

Research from Xerox shows that personalised digital print can increase response rate by as much as 30%, which in turn reduces lead acquisition costs and boosts your bottom line!

Here are a few ways clients of mine have used Personalisation Power:

• Direct mail to prospects

• Brochures to existing customers with personal front covers

• New Product launches

• Personal website addresses e.g. www.yourcompanyname.com/jamessmith

• Personalised website sales or landing pages

• Newsletters

• Loyalty marketing

For expert advice and great customer service in this area contact an award-winning client of mine, Banbury Litho.

Visit **www.banburylitho.co.uk** or call 01295 220 488 – 10% off your first order when you mention this book or ask for their FREE report into how you can save money on your printing.

Buy my Turbo Marketing DVD

To learn more powerful, proven, profit-building marketing strategies, own my Turbo Marketing DVD now by visiting

www.TurboMarketing.Biz

Here are just 7 of the Key Topics I cover on this DVD:

1. The 5 biggest marketing mistakes businesses make and how to fix them...

2. The 1 area you must invest 60% of your marketing in to succeed...

3. How to plan your marketing campaigns for maximum profits...

4. The 3 critical components of a successful marketing campaign...

5. The No1 skill you must master to become a successful marketer...

6. The 4 marketing components of The Business Engine™ and how to use them to drive your business growth...

7. How to increase the Life Time Value of your customers...

Own it today and see your marketing results skyrocket!

Join a Proactive Networking Group

I've often said, "The size of your network determines the level of your net worth", so if you want to increase your business, get out of bed and get networking.

My experience with my own networking club, The Oxford Wealth Club **www.Wealth-Club.Biz** now in it's 5th year, is that those members who commit to it as a strategy, attend regular meetings and focus on helping other businesses in the group, get back far more than they take out. Those who attend just to try a hit and run sales approach never last and never reap the benefits.

You have to invest time in building credibility and trust with the group but, when you have, the business will flood in. After all, a referred sales lead is likely to have a far higher conversion rate, in some cases over 75%!

Here's what happened for two of our members, one a new member in his first year and another just starting their fourth year and the results they're both getting:

Client Case Studies

"Since joining the Oxford Wealth Club we're received leads resulting in over £20,000 of new business in just 6 months."

— Graham (MD), INCA, The Caring Accountants

"We renewed for our 3rd year at Wealth Club not only because it is a fantastic resource for knowledge, energy and business growth – because it also pays for itself and our time over and over with the business we continue to do with members and contacts made over breakfast."

— James (MD), Get Support www.getsupport.com

Just a little word of warning, keep asking yourself, am I Networking – or Netbreakfasting?

Action Steps:

Now take a moment to list the top three strategies from this chapter you will implement.

1 ....

....

....

....

2. ....

....

....

....

3. ....

....

....

....

If you have any questions on this chapter...

Go to **www.AskPaulAvins.com** and ask me!

"Win not by surviving the storm,
but by changing the game"

— Sam Palmisano (Chairman and CEO of IBM)

Chapter 4:

Website Sales and Marketing

"There is no limit to the amount of money people will find for things they WANT on-line."

— Frank Kern, Internet Marketing Guru

Using the Ever-Growing Internet to your Benefit

For most products or services today, 85% of all buying is initiated on the Internet (if only for research). On-line sales are predicted to grow by 14% in 2009 – even in a recession.

When you boil it down there are two critical areas you must master to build a successful and profitable on-line business or on-line section to your business.

- Targeted Traffic Generation – getting the right prospects to your web site

- Converting visitors into customers – making the sale!

In my experience too many business owners focus too much attention on just getting traffic, any traffic, in the hope of making money.

THIS IS A WASTE OF TIME & MONEY

Remember: nothing happens in a business until somebody buys something for a profit, whether on-line or offline.

Focus on building trust with your prospects and customers. Make sure that they need do no more than 3 clicks from the time they arrive at your site, to the point they can purchase.

Always keep asking yourself – "What do I want my visitor to do next?" and "How can I make this easier and quicker for them?"

Get an "outsider" to check your website for you and give you real visitor feedback. The results may surprise you.!

Make sure Google Analytics is Installed and Monitored

If you don't have this installed on your web site get it ASAP. Not only is it amazing software but it is also free – yes, FREE!. Just go to the Google home page or ask your web developer to set it up for you.

This software will give you a full dashboard of just how well, or poorly, your website is performing. Once you know where people are going and what they are doing you can start to improve the sales process. Focus on these metrics:

- The home page bounce rate (number of visitors jumping right back out as it's not what they hoped for)

- Number of Unique visitors per week / month

- Number of pages visited

- Highest exit page – why?

- Shopping Carts abandoned

- Highest referring keywords

Start using PPC to Drive more Targeted Traffic

Although for some industries PPC (Pay Per Click) is starting to get expensive, the fact that 14% of people regularly click on them means you can get very targeted traffic to your web site for a lot less than traditional advertising. This is why it makes it a great option for small to medium sized businesses.

You can set it up in just a few minutes, track exactly what results you get and set a maximum budget so you have total control over your costs.

No wonder marketers love it! Take action and get started today even if it is just with £100 to see what results you achieve.

Offer an "Ethical Bribe" so Visitors will give you their e-mail Address

If you are doing business on-line you should be building your e-mail database in a legal way. Never buy e-mail lists and send SPAM as your e-mail account might be suspended and could even be shut down.

The best way to get people to join your e-mail database is to offer them a FREE gift or bonus for giving you "permission" to talk to them via e-mail.

The better the bonus the higher the sign up. Here are a few you could try:

- Free E-book

- Special Report

- Free MP3 interview

- Tips booklet

- A discount voucher

- Free Newsletter

- E-Course

- Free CD

- Product sample

- Ticket for an event

Make sure you promote this on your Home Page and have the joining box clearly marked.

Create Targeted Landing Pages

In the previous marketing section, I talked about getting the right message to match your market to increase the response rate of your offline activity. On-line this is even more important because people typically give you fewer than 5 seconds to capture their attention before they click off and are gone forever.

Create a number of individual, targeted landing pages, (by this I mean the first page a prospect experiences on your site), which use the words that hit the reader's hot buttons. This strategy is powerful when linked with Pay Per Click. For instance, when people click on an advert for weight-loss products and come to a page using emotion evoking phrases such as "fast and effective weight loss" backed up with testimonials together with before and after pictures. However these very same products could also have a separate landing page aimed at the fitness market using different exercise and toning language to excite them into buying. We have just doubled our potential market and made sales go up!

Add "the Human Touch" to your Website

The biggest challenge with an on-line business is that it may be open 24 hours but lacks that human interaction people subconsciously crave before placing orders.

There is new technology you can add to your site that enables your customers to type any questions they may have into a "Chat" box with a live operator. This adds the *human* element and gives you insights into what your prospects are really thinking or feeling.

A recent survey showed that these "Chat" boxes increased conversion rates by 18% when added to web sites and this is with no more effort. In fact, it greatly reduced abandoned shopping carts because when people either got confused or had a question they wanted answering before they parted with their money – they could use the box.

Free Bonus

I've arranged for you to have access to a FREE 50 minute on-line video where one of the world's leading experts in this area explains how it can have a huge impact on your bottom line.

Simply go to **www.Paul-Avins.com/chatvideo**

This video is valued at £95 but is FREE to you as a *thank you* for buying this book.

Use Auto-Responders to Automatically Follow Up with People

It still amazes me how many companies never respond to e-mail requests for quotes for their products or services. Perhaps they have too much business already, but I doubt it!

Today there is an abundance of software that can be purchased for less than £100 that will enable you to fully automate regular communication with your past customers or visitors who "opt in" to join your e-mail newsletter etc.

Remember: one of the challenges in this recession economy is that people need more follow up, not less. More regular contact, not less, and more special offers to keep your tills ringing.

Cure follow-up fatigue today by implementing this into your business before your competitors do.

Work with an SEO (Search Engine Optimisation) Company to Drive Organic Traffic

Over 80% of all searches in the UK are made on Google which is a huge source of potential business for you.

In fact, conversion rates are a significant 17% higher for organic traffic than for Pay Per Click traffic, and searchers are up to 6 times more likely to click on the first few organic results than any of the PPC adverts.

Now, this area is a "black art" in itself and I'm definitely not an expert but you do need to get the right advice from someone who is, preferably with 3 or more years of experience with SMEs and who is up-to-date with all the latest strategies.

You'll need to consider your site structure and the web copy, which works in a different way to copy for print, as well as thinking about things such as the number of links to your site and keyword choice.

There is a fantastic FREE report you can download at **www.momentumws.co.uk/spotlight** which will set you off in the right direction.

Use Video Testimonials & Demonstrations of your Products

Video increases sales, it's that simple! And with faster broadband and better video players being rolled out more and more we are entering the age of Web TV.

Think about it – TV advertising has built huge companies, but traditionally you always needed a lot of money to play the game. Not anymore, you don't! On-line, your potential customers are more sceptical of you. There is a lack of trust as they look to answer the question "Does their product or service really do what they claim?"

Provide social proof to sceptical prospects by adding video testimonials to your website. What I mean by this is that they will be reassured by viewing real people who are already happy with your products or services. All you need is a Flip Video Camera from any good on-line electrical retailer (approximately £89) and you are good to go. For a great fun example of how to use video to promote a product visit **www.willitblend.com** - their video clips catapulted sales and eventually went viral on YouTube.com.

Claim Your Free Internet Marketing DVD

(valued at £29) visit www.paul-avins.com/FreeDVD

Turn "Dead Space into Profit Space"

This is a great *off line* strategy that can really deliver on-line. Go through your web site and look at areas where there may be blank space on low priority pages.

For example, some e-commerce sites will take customers to a "thank you for your order" page, but they so often fail to add a new special offer here to boost sales.

What other dead spaces could you turn into streams of income?

Check your web site pages – NOW!

Set up an e-Newsletter

Yes, I agree, there are more and more of these about. However, IF you make it content-rich and IF you come from a point of view of adding value rather than just trying to sell to people – then they still work.

Put a "Sign-Up for my Newsletter" box on every page of your web site and even offer a bonus or ethical bribe to encourage potential customers to join.

The focus is on adding value and building a relationship – the sales will come, and more quickly than you think.

Use Joint Ventures to Drive Qualified Traffic

This can be a huge source of profits and sales for you. All you need to do is find other non-competing on-line businesses that sell to your specific target market. Then offer them a commission to promote your product or service to their customers. The power of their endorsement to a customer list they have already built trust with over the years will deliver a much higher return than an offer to a cold list.

Now, you'll have to demonstrate your commitment to looking after their reputation and their customers, and it goes without saying that the product or service must be good, but with all these factors in place this can be a very fast and effective way to win-win profits.

Who do you already know who sells to your market place that you could call and offer this type of opportunity to? Find out now – and do it!

Sponsor other People's e-Newsletters

Again, a very quick and cost-effective way to get to potential customers in your target market.

Simply identify non-competing businesses, as you have done for Joint Ventures, and ask to sponsor their e-newsletters.

Most people will be happy to let you do this for a couple of hundred pounds at the most, and you get your message in front of some very targeted readers.

Make sure you have full tracking on the click-through numbers and sales made from this type of campaign, so you can evaluate your Return on Investment (ROI) and judge whether it is worth doing again.

Get People to User-test your Site

Quite often we are so close to our own businesses or web sites that we are no longer able to see them through the eyes of our new visitors. After all, we have probably been looking at our web pages for weeks and weeks, if not longer!

It's a good idea to ask friends and family or even students to conduct some user testing on your site. Get a commitment from them to be

100% honest in their feedback – this is no time to be nice. Pay them for their time if you have to, as the learning you'll get could lead to changes that will improve your visitors' experience, and should increase your sales.

It's no time to get precious about your site – it's time to get honest and fix what's not working so you and the business can move forward.

Use Affiliates to Drive Traffic and Sales to your Site

I just love this strategy as, rather than paying just for click through, page impressions or traffic from a search engine, you are paying for RESULTS! In short, sales.

Simply put, you offer other websites the chance to sell your products for a commission, that only gets paid when people they refer buy from you, and the cash is in your hands. The higher the percentage commission, the more effort they tend to put into selling your product.

Client Story

A website retail client of mine used this strategy to cut his Adwords spend by 85% (£6.5k per month / £78k per year) and still boosted sales by 15% at the same time. A real win win result!

Don't worry if you are not technical there are companies set up to do all the tracking and in some cases manage the payments as well for you. Just search for them under "Affiliate suppliers". Remember no downside here just sales

Start using Social Media Sites to raise your Profile and Drive Traffic to your Website.

We could write a whole book on this topic and many people have done! The key to remember is that Social networking is about PEOPLE and about building a RELATIONSHIP of trust over time. In fact it's the anti sales approach. The less you sell the more people like and trust you, so the more they buy! Grasp this and you are 95% ahead of other business owners.

Here are some of the main social sites you should look into being on: LinkedIn, Twitter, Facebook, Delicious, Flickr, & YouTube. A great and easy to use tool is Ping.fm or Utterli.com to post one update that will appear across all of your network of social sites at once, and save you time and the 'headache' of doing it one by one!

What I would say is that you need to work out how much time you have to invest in building a following (or "tribe" as Marketing legend Seth Godin calls it), then pick the best location where your customers and prospects are likely to congregate and start a dialogue with them. Get involved in the conversation

For example LinkedIn is a place to connect with professional people, and the best place to promote your company, Facebook is primarily for your family and friends etc.

You can connect with me at **www.linkedin.com/in/paulavins** or **www.facebook.com/paulavins.**

Blogging for Business

Research has shown that blogs are consistently some of the most viewed content online. This can be very effective especially if you operate in a defined niche where you can build a blog of high quality content of REAL value to the readers, and it's a great way to showcase you knowledge and expertise.

A word of warning though, once you start you MUST keep it up. Schedule updating as a regular activity in your weekly diary, you must blog at least two to three times a week in order for your blog to be considered a viable and legitimate blog. Keep that in mind as you start your journey into social media marketing. If you have a website that doesn't offer a blog component, consider WordPress as a Free solution. It's easy to install and simple to use. **www.wordpress.com**.

You can read my Blog at **www.PaulAvinsBlog.com** to find out what I'm up to and to learn more great tools to boost your profits or visit **www.paul-avins.com/sosblog** and see what people are saying about this book!

If you're just starting out you may want to consider using Twitter which is 'micro blogging' as you can only post 140 characters. It's a great way to keep in touch and constantly update people about what's happening in your business. Visit **www.twitter.com** to set up your page and be sure to follow me by visiting **www.twitterpaulavins.com**. Make sure it's linked back to your site as Google loves all fresh content so it helps Search Engine Optimisation

Read my Blog at **www.PaulAvinsBlog.com**.

Action Steps:

Now take a moment to list the top three strategies from this chapter you will implement.

1...

....

....

....

....

2. ....

....

....

....

3. ....

....

....

....

If you have any questions on this chapter...

Go to **www.AskPaulAvins.com** and ask me!

"A decision to omit social media
from your business model is a
decision to surrender market share
to your competitor."

— Ron Davies, Social Media Marketing Expert

Chapter 5:

Sales

> *"If you don't have a system for selling, you are at the mercy of your customers' system for buying"*
>
> — David Sandler, Sales Trainer

Selling Never Ends

People often say that nothing happens in business until a sale gets made (for a profit), and that great sales people build companies. In reality, of course, we are all selling all the time.

Whether it's selling the bank on extending our overdraft, selling a supplier on giving us a discount, selling a team member on the benefits to them of going the extra mile for the customer, we are all in the sales business all the time.

Unfortunately, because there have been so many sales people who either just did not understand how to treat potential customers or who were trained in the old "pressure, sell and run" approach, selling as a profession has got a bad name.

If you want to succeed on a LARGE scale then not only do you have to learn to master this critical skill, you need to love playing the sales game.

In this chapter, I've pulled together strategies you can use if you yourself do all the selling, as well as strategies you can use to build a sales team - and this is something which will need to happen for you to grow and expand.

Remember: selling is helping people with problems and challenges to see if your solutions solve their needs. If it does, then you have a customer and they have a new trusted adviser on their team!

Client Case Study

"My business grew from £650,000 to over £3.9 million in just over 3 years! Paul's Sales and Business Coaching has delivered real results for me."

— David Kirby (MD), Concept Plc

Get Closer to your Bigger Clients

Larger customers whose business accounts form anything over 20% of your turnover can be a mixed blessing. It's great to have this turnover, but the loss of this one client could be catastrophic to your business. So don't take them for granted! If you lose such a client it can take months, if not years, to replace them and right now they'll be prime targets for your competitors. So get close to them – closer than ever before.

- Add more value to your service.

- Give them loyalty bonuses they don't expect out of the blue, they could be free.

Use corporate hospitality or social events to build a more rounded relationship with them.

Think about it this way, if you want a £1 million customer you have to build a £1 million relationship.

Divert 50% of your Time and Energy Currently spent Selling to NEW Customers to Selling More to your EXISTING Customers

Harry Mills, in his book The Rain Makers Toolkit, published by Amacon ISBN: 9780814472163 studied sales people's conversion rates and this is the result:

- New Prospects – 1 out of 8 converted to a sale

- Inactive past customers – 1 out of 3 converted to a sale

- Active Clients – 1 in every 2 converted to a sale

So if you shift half your selling time to inactive past customers or active customers who could buy other products and services you offer, your results will JUMP by as much as 300/400% – with no more effort!

Better Qualification of your Buyers and Potential Customers

Make sure that all your appointments are with authorized decision makers and buyers. So much time is wasted travelling to see prospects who don't have this authority, and it not only wastes time and money, but it can be a huge demotivator to your sales teams.

FEAR stops people qualifying hard prospects – but you need to start respecting your time more. After all, when today is over it's gone for... good!

Questions to ask:

- If what I show you makes commercial sense – do you have the budget to purchase it this month/quarter?

- Who else do you like to get involved in making decisions about a purchase of this type? – (This will flush out influencers and other decision-makers)

They may not always tell you the answers, but if you never ask you'll never know.

Carry and Use Client Testimonials and Case Studies

We all feel nervous before handing over our hard-earned cash to a new supplier who promises to solve our problems. We have doubts. Will they deliver? How do I know I can trust them? Will the product do what they claim?

As suppliers to our worried potential customers we need to reassure them with something more than just words – they want to see proof.

Not just any proof, but *Social Proof* that other people just like them used what you offer and got the results they desired.

The Solution? Lots and lots and lots of client testimonials and case studies.

Life Saving Tips:

- Carry paper copies of testimonials, preferably on your clients' headed paper for credibility, to all sales appointments.

- Use a picture of the client as well for further proof. You can never have too many – take what you have and multiply it by 10.

- Get Video testimonials if you can. An easy way is using a Flip Video recorder (approx. £89.00).

- Make sure your testimonial clients talk in detail about the specific issue or problem they had before your arrival and the specific results, with financial impact if applicable, that you have helped them achieve.

Speed up your Quoting Response Time

Dan Kennedy, the US author of No BS Marketing, published by Entrepreneur Press ISBN: 9781599181813 Consultant and Speaker, is fond of saying "Money loves Speed". I can show you client data that PROVES that the faster you respond to an enquiry or quote request the greater your chance of winning the order.

Some steps to follow:

- Measure your current quote response time – this often surprises business owners as it's frequently far slower than they think.

- Document your quoting process and see what procedures can be streamlined or removed altogether.

- Use technology to help speed up the process – quotation software is available for all types of industry or use Excel sheets with locked-down formulas.

- Keep measuring the time taken and asking – how can we respond even more quickly?

Client Story

When one of my clients who was a Private Investigator did this his conversion rate more than doubled – up from 13% to 30% in just 12-months! That's a lot of sales!

Ask, ask, ask for the Order!

Over the years I have run sales teams of various sizes from three to over one hundred and the one thing which really shocked me when I went on appointments with them – how many of them never asked for the order! They would give good quality presentations, build great rapport with the prospect – but never ask for the order. Can you believe that!

Research done by IBM many years ago showed that prospects will say "No" up to 7 times before they say "Yes". Consider that most sales people never even ask once and that those who do only ask once – just how much money is being left on the table?

Make a commitment to get good at asking for the order. Guess what, your prospects expect you to, after all it's your job to do so! If you wait for them to order you're not a sales person, you're an order taker!

Work out one or two simple phrases you feel comfortable with and just use them over and over again.

I have seen sales people get great results with a simple phrase such as:

"Shall I outline what we need to do to get you started?"

Write down your closing question and commit to start using it today!

My new closing question is:

....

....

....

....

....

....

....

....

Implement a more Process-driven Follow up Programme

If you invest in any type of marketing to generate lead and then invest nothing in designing a follow-up system that stays in touch with that prospect, you are throwing SO MUCH money down the drain, it hurts!

After all, if people have requested a quote from you, they must be interested in what you have to offer. It might not be right now, but at some point they will buy.

Here are a few key ideas to implement:

- Have a regular time blocked out in your diary to follow up – make it a team activity if possible and have fun with prizes for top sales.

- Put prospects on an e-mail, newsletter and call cycle so they get contacted at least every 30 days until they buy.

- Invest in a database or CRM (Contact Resorce Management) system (ACT, Salesforce.com, Goldmine etc) which will track prospects and can prompt you to contact them again. This software can now be bought on a monthly subscription basis and will pay for itself if used correctly.

Key Idea: Implement a **Follow Up Friday™** twice a month to stay on top of outstanding quotes.

Put Sales Targets on Display in Your Office for All to See!

It amazes me how many business owners don't set targets, and those that do think it's best to keep the team in the dark about them!

WRONG! After all if you didn't know the score in a game of football, how long would you keep playing or watching – not very long, I would suggest. So get everybody involved and make it fun. Just seeing how close you are to hitting a target will inspire people to push that little bit harder every month – especially if there is a bonus for them.

One of my clients, an Interior Designer, made a *Blue Peter* style colourful target thermometer with her team and stuck it on the wall opposite the office door so everybody saw it when they came in and out. Not surprisingly they are growing like crazy, up over 50% – and in a tough housing market as well!

Questions to answer:

- What could you do to get your team more involved in "owning" the sales target?

....

....

....

....

....

- How could you make the process more fun?

....

....

....

....

....

- Where could you put your target indicator so everybody can see it?

....

....

- When will you implement it?

   Target date:...

Build more Rapport

Research shows that in sales situations potential customers buy from people they KNOW, LIKE and TRUST – and from people they feel are like THEMSELVES.

So if you don't take time to truly get to know your prospect you are seriously jeopardising any chance you have of making a sale, now or in the future.

Simple SOS Sales steps to build more rapport:

• Listen more than talk (2 ears 1 mouth – use them accordingly). Over 65% of sales people talk themselves out of more business than they win.

• Study body language and NLP (neuro-linguistic programming – a system designed to educate people in self-awareness and effective communication) for example, matching and mirroring your customer and their language can immensely improve your rapport and therefore conversion levels.

• Find out about your customer's family, hobbies, journey to this point in their career or business – look for similarities in your own life to connect.

• Dress appropriately – don't look like a banker or tax man, but don't be so casual that you won't be taken seriously. Go for one level above what your customer usually wears.

Know your Conversion Rate and Set a Goal to Increase It

This is a critical number that all business owners, sales people and sales managers should know. After all, if you don't know what it is how can you ever hope to improve it?

It's easy to monitor. Simply track the number of quotes you send out or the number of visitors that come into your shop or visit your web site. Then divide this figure by the number of sales you make and you have your conversion rate. If it's way over 50% then chances are you're too cheap and you can put your prices up!

If it's less than 30% you need to upgrade your sales skills because there is room for improvement!

Once you know what your conversion rate is, set a goal to increase it. This strategy is all about being and working smarter, not working harder. More skill and less effort.

Stop Closing Sales and Start Opening Relationships

If you want a £50,000 client you have to build a £50,000 relationship with them. The days of pressure selling are over. Customers are more sophisticated and more informed due to the Internet and are looking for *trusted advisers* to help them navigate the data and information overload.

All your prospects and customers have personal emotional bank accounts. When you listen to them, get to know them, ask questions – you are making deposits. Without these deposits it's impossible for you to make a withdrawal (The Sale).

Key Idea: Stop making sales just to get a customer and start getting customers to make more sales.

> *"People don't care how much you know until they know how much you care"*
> — John Maxwell, author.

Go Back to all Your Past Customers or Unconverted Leads

Some of your past customers and unconverted leads may be at death's door but you can still breathe life back into them!

- Create a reactivation plan - an electrifying offer to shock them back to life!

- Follow up cold leads and ask what stopped them ordering before?

- Communicate more frequently with them through e-mails, newsletters, case studies, etc.

Client Story

A coaching client of mine recently used this easy-to-implement strategy to generate over £4,000 in sales from just a couple of e-mails sent to a list of prospects she thought were dead!!

Imagine what that would do to her bottom line if she did it every month! A prospect is never dead until they stop breathing...

Do More Sales Training with Your Team

As the old saying goes, "The more you Learn the more you Earn" and sales skills get blunted by rejection and negativity faster than most.

Introduce short 30 minute training sessions with your team to kick the week off. Give everybody sales training CDs to listen to in their car turning dead time into learning time. Introduce a book of the month program.

A salesperson I knew used to commit to 5 hours per week just reading and listening to CDs and saw his conversion rate go from 22% to 96% in just over 18 months.

Just think about how profitable that learning time turned out to be!

Commit to buying books and CDs and listen to them in the car. You can always start with my products which you can find at

www.paul-avins.com (Remember to always ask for the sale, I practice what I preach!)

Client Story

"I have been running monthly Sales Training teleconference calls for a client of mine for the last 6 months. Recovering the key principles in the sales process. Robert Bruce (Director) "it's been very positive and powerful" the result is a 31% increase in sales year to date."

— SOS Action Step – Plan in a sales training session today...

Set a Goal to Double Your Sales then Figure Out How You Do It

Our brains are very powerful super computers of which we use less than 5% of their true potential. Too often we forget that our role is to ask our brain powerful questions then to focus on the creative answers it generates. When you use the *power of intention* it's amazing the type of opportunities you start to see everywhere. So ....

How could you double your business in the next 12-months if your life depended on it? (In this climate it very well may!)

Tip: Keep a pad and pen by your bed, as many of these ideas will pop into your head when you least expect them, or when your brain is fresh in the morning.

When you come up with an idea, take action on it, talk about it, talk to your team and get their reactions. Test and measure your results on a small scale first – if it works then GO LARGE!

Divide Your Customers into the Top 20%

This harnesses the power of the 80/20 rule that says 80% of your results come from 20% of your activity, but in a different way. List your customers by profit, highest first then work down. Divide up the top 20%, then divide up the next 20% block. Work out how much profit you would generate if you moved this block up to the same levels as the top 20% and go to work to sell them more of your profitable products and services.

Warning! This strategy looks deceptively simple yet can grow your sales by hundreds of % with a lot less effort than is needed focusing on getting new business.

Don't Give Cash Discounts
— Give Bonuses or Gifts to Close a Sale

This strategy also appears in the Profit section but for different reasons.

Think about it this way...

If you have a customer who will not commit to a £5,000 order until you give them a 10% (or more) discount you'd be giving away £500 cash, which, if you have a 20% gross margin, is 50% of your margin!

However, if you were to offer him, say an £800 perceived value alternative that only costs you £300 then you've saved yourself £2300 cash over the discount deal – a real win-win deal which will cut down conversion times as it looks like a better deal than the customer originally wanted.

Estee Lauder Cosmetics is generally credited with creating the "gift-with-purchase" concept that operates in the high end retail market and it generates millions of pounds in sales and profits every year,

High perceived value products or services can also include:

• Memberships

• Consultancy time

• Extended service contracts

• Additional warranties

• Information products, e-books / reports etc

• Products being discontinued

What can you start doing in your business today?

....

....

....

....

....

....

Document Your Existing Sales Process

Very few businesses ever do this in my experience of coaching. So it's hardly surprising that cracks appear and prospects and sales slip through them without anybody ever noticing.

It's easy to get the system started – take a large sheet of flip-chart paper and create a flow chart to monitor the process of the enquiry from the time a prospect contacts you until the time they buy from you.

Start working on these next questions – quickly!

Look at your sales process and ask yourself:

- What areas need to be expanded on?

....

....

....

....

- What areas need to be streamlined?

....

....

....

....

- What needs to be removed all together?

....

....

....

....

- What areas could be improved?

....

....

....

....

Know and Monitor Your AOV (Average Order Value)

This is a MUST. If you don't know it right now, go back and work it out.

Total divided by the number of orders = AOV

Just by monitoring it you'll find the AOV goes up but you must set a target to stretch for – why not go for doubling it?

Checklists are just one way you can boost this number.

Implement Checklists to Help Sales People Up-Sell More Effectively

This is a quick cash strategy that takes a couple of hours to set up but will start generating additional sales and profits right away!

Look at your CORE product or service lines – then look at all the products or services that "link" off them that a customer could and may buy, but often forgets or just does not think about.

For example:

I have a client who sells insurance. If you buy Business Premises Insurance from him, he'll also ask you about:

• Your fleet insurance for vehicles

• Business travel insurance

• Health insurance

He actually has over 20 different products he can offer you which represents 20 opportunities to make a sale.

Introduce a Customer Loyalty Scheme

Once you have won the trust of a new customer the goal of every business must be to keep that customer buying from them for as long as possible – also known as the Life Time Value (LTV).

Human beings have a simple response mechanism. If you praise them for doing something, they do more of it. If you reward them with something tangible, that they value, they will do more of what got them the reward.

Loyalty schemes utilize this fact and if they are delivered correctly they can be hugely successful, as the Tesco Club card model shows.

The key point here is that you want to make PROFITABLE customers loyal and unprofitable customers made profitable by offering rewards!

Here are some points to remember when setting up your own loyalty scheme:

- It is a long-term commitment so don't start it for a short term hit.

- Make sure everybody in your business is trained in how it works before offering it to your customers.

- Test it with a small number of customers first, perhaps in just one location if possible.

- Remember – this strategy won't overcome the fact that you have poor products or poor customer service.

- Make sure they get something physical for joining – e.g. card or welcome pack, etc.

Offer Upgrade and Trade-in Options to Past Customers

This is a very quick but very powerful tool to drive your sales right now. Technology moves so fast that products are outdated very quickly and if you offer people an opportunity to trade in and trade up their old for new, the results can be huge.

A good offer would be to give an upgraded model/product/ service for the same price as last time which would be cheaper than offering a discount.

Client Story

When I did this with one of my coaching clients, he generated over £250,000 in additional sales within 7 days of the mail shot being sent out!

This strategy is used very effectively by Mobile Phone Companies, The Motor Industry and even house builders who offer to take your old home in part exchange!

List below the ways you could use upgrades and trade-ins in your business to grow sales:

....

....

....

....

....

....

....

....

....

....

....

....

....

....

10 X ROI Factor (Return On Investment)

In these more cost-conscious times, buyers need to be more convinced than ever before that the money they invest in your product or service will deliver them a significant Return On their Investment (ROI).

If you can only demonstrate a return of two or three times over the life of your product or service, then the harsh reality is that people will hang onto their cash. You must find a way to get it close to x 10 ROI factor if you want those wallets or budgets to open up.

ROIs can be demonstrated to your prospect in 3 different ways:

• Increase in sales or profits

• Reduction in operating costs

• Increase in productivity / time saving

Make sure you understand how to calculate and demonstrate for maximum impact.

Build Your Credibility

Prospects are harder to impress today than ever before and they want to buy from the suppliers they perceive as experts in their field.

The battle has shifted to that of credibility. Here facts play a key part and every business has some they can use.

So, how can you convince a customer of your credibility?

Ask yourself these SOS questions:

• How long have I been in business?

....

• How many customers have I served since I started?

....

• How many Industry Awards have I won?

....

....

....

....

• What Industry bodies am I a member of?

....

....

....

....

• Do I have ISO, Investors in People or other accreditations?

....

....

....

....

If you are still struggling get creative!

- Write a book or Publish a White Paper (can be as short as 6 pages). See a great example at **www.presentationparadox.com**.

- Write advertorials and publish them often.

- Think outside the box – a stationery client of mine tells people they sell enough paper clips a year to go round the world 5 times. It really gets peoples attention!

- Get a local business celebrity to endorse your product or service.

Credibility builds trust and trust makes sales happen.

Set Clear Outcome Goals

We've all seen the stressed-out sales person rushing into a building having dumped their dirty car in the car park with papers falling out of their brief case. They have no plan, in fact it's a miracle they made it to the meeting at all! With this approach, what are their chances of making the sale?

Arrive early for sales meetings. Turn off your phone. Take 5 minutes to work out your goals for the meeting, then relax and visualise a successful meeting. When you do this and review it afterwards you'll be amazed how often you get the outcome you wanted.

Promise Small and Deliver BIG

The No1 sin a sales person can commit is to over-sell the benefits or capabilities of their product or service, as it's just setting the business up to fail. Prospects would always prefer you only to promise what you can guarantee to deliver – then WOW them by delivering far more than they expected. This creates a raving fan and somebody who will refer others to you or promote you on their Blog, which is free marketing. Customers have emotional bank accounts and when you let them down by over promising, you make a big withdrawal.

Implement a Proactive Customer Referral System (CRS)

The reality is that people like to be around people like themselves, and research shows that even a boring person knows over 250 people well enough to introduce you to them!

The key point here is that, because of their independent nature, referrals are a very low-cost, powerful marketing strategy and they will convert at a much higher level than any other type of lead. In fact, it's the fastest, easiest way to DOUBLE your business. Just get every one of your customers to refer you to one more customer just like them – how easy was that? However, a quick warning - if you don't frame up new customers to give you referrals it's harder to go back and ask them for these later, and most people never ask for them which is just plain crazy.

Here are a few ways you can get more referrals:

- Make it a condition of doing business with you. I tell all my new clients that once we have begun to see significant improvement in their own business – I will expect them to refer me to others within their network.

- Have a system for asking for them during the "honeymoon" period.

- Offer a referral fee or reward.

- Use technology to make it easy for people to recommend you.

- Ask for help meeting specific people in your town rather than just asking for a list of "referrals" which is too big a task for most people to comprehend.

- Monitor how many you get and set a goal to double it.

What is the first step you need to take to implement this in your business right now?

....

....

Action Steps:

Now take a moment to list the top three strategies from this chapter you will implement.

1 ....

....

....

2. ....

....

....

3. ....

....

....

If you have any questions on this chapter...

Go to **www.AskPaulAvins.com** and ask me!

Chapter 6:

Cash Flow

> "You have to withstand pressure. If you can't handle pressure you can't be a great or successful entrepreneur."
>
> — Donald Trump

Cash is Everything!

As many business people have said over the years, "Turnover is Vanity – Profit is Reality", and in times of recession, Cash is not just King – it's EVERYTHING!

The fact is that with banks trying to rebuild their own balance sheets by calling in overdrafts from so many businesses, you no longer have the security of knowing that if people take longer to pay you can just run in overdraft. The game has well and truly changed.

This is the No1 topic with many of my personal coaching clients right now, and what I'm going to share with you are strategies that have been working in today's world, not in a world where credit was easy to get.

Use some or all of them and you'll thrive while others struggle to survive, but always remember this... more businesses go bust because of a lack of cash than because of a lack of profitability. However much time you think you have when the cash starts to dry up – you have at lest 50% of that in reality, and you must act with speed.

Cash flow management is one of the critical skills you must master as a business owner, or you'll pay a heavy price. And, in my experience, a lack of cash flow generates the greatest pressure you can ever feel as an entrepreneur.

Client Case Study

"Recently Paul helped me get back into a more positive mindset and within just a few weeks of my session with Paul I had released an additional £65,000 cash into my new business"

— Rachel Elnaugh, Original BBC2 Dragon from Dragons Den

Set a Goal to Reduce all Operating Costs

This is a strategy that affects both your cash flow and profits and will have a compound effect over the next 12 months.

The best way to approach this is by breaking down all your costs and taking them as a % of total costs. This will show you where the largest cost areas are, then you can start with these. If your sales have fallen by, say, 30%, then you need to cut your costs by at least the same amount to stay in balance, even if you have money in the bank.

Be tough – ask yourself if you really need everything you currently buy?

Renegotiate every contract, rent, phones, vehicles, etc.

If you have to make redundancies do it fast, within the law and be decisive. Explain to those left behind why it was needed and what they need to do to ensure there are not any more.

Set up Credit Limits for all Customers and Monitor Closely

Here are 4 things to consider to monitor
your creditors:

- Hold regular scheduled finance meetings with
  your team

- Monitor risky accounts and reduce their credit limits

- Act quickly if you feel somebody may go bust on you

- Consider taking out credit insurance

Remember: you are not your customers' bank, so don't let them treat you like one. Also, the longer a debt remains unpaid the harder it is to get it paid. Make sure you have an escalation process in place to turn up the heat on non-payers.

Make sure you keep talking to non-payers as when the communication stops that's when the biggest risk to your money occurs.

Plan Large Purchases around VAT / Tax Due Dates to Maximize Offsets and Cash Outflow

This strategy just requires you to know your VAT quarter dates and work with them instead of just buying whenever you feel like it.

Become aware of when the beginning of the quarter is and make sure any large purchases are right near the end so you're not carrying the VAT obligation for up to 90 days.

Client Story

One client of mine had a regular supplier bill him for a 12-month project at the start with a monthly payment plan but it meant they could claim all the VAT back on the year in one go which helped them with cash flow in the short term.

Remember: you can negotiate payment terms for large VAT and Corporation tax bills. The Government is now more understanding than ever about the pressures on business, but if you don't ask you'll not get, and you must do it BEFORE the bill due date.

Change Your Terms & Conditions

Too many business owners just set up their terms and conditions based on what everybody else in their industry does, but you can set them up to work for your business from day one.

The goal here is to give you CASH as soon as possible so you can stay liquid and pay suppliers as needed.

Depending on the type of business you run, here are some simple yet very powerful strategies that will help to maximize the flow of cash to you now:

Service Businesses:

• Money on Account or Payment Plan

• Standing Order or Direct Debit for regular payments

• Cash up Front

• Staged Payments on project milestones – make sure that agreed payments are maintained

Product Business:

- Payment with order (shops have been doing it for years!)

- Staged Payments, e.g. during build phase

- Split payment, eg. 50% with order, 25% when shipped, when 25% on completion.

This strategy is also in the Profit section but for a slightly different reason.

Implement a Sales Pipeline

This is a critical part of your cash flow planning system. It involves forecasting your likely sales for, say, the next 90 days. It won't be 100% accurate, but it will enable you to plan production and delivery resources and give you some idea of what your cash flow might be. After all, if you have no idea what sales are heading your way how can you work out how many more you need to stay afloat?

If you are in a reactive business where sales come to you, such as retail or e-tail, then you need to see how much up or down you are on last year as a percentage, then project that forward for a rolling 90 days based on last year's numbers.

For Example:

If you were 25% down year to date and last year's figures were:

April / May / June 08

£250k / £200K / £225K

Then your cash flow projection would be based on sales of:

April / May / June / 09

£156k / £150k / £168k

I would also suggest a weekly sales meeting with your team to review the progress of what's in the pipeline as it's your early warning system for future cash flow problems.

Increase Your Conversion Rate

The easiest way to generate cash flow fast is to increase sales. I've covered this in much more detail in the Sales section but here are just a few of my top ideas that you can implement quickly and which will help:

- Answer the phone faster and more professionally

- Have every team member take customer service and basic sales training

- Increase your speed of response to enquiries

- Ask for the order more often

- Put a Guarantee in place

- Follow up all past unsold leads

- Offer discounts or one-off bonuses for payments up front

- Use more testimonials & case studies

- Set realistic but stretching sales targets

- Study Sales CDs and Books

Cross-sell and Up-sell More

This is EASY, quick cash and again there is more detail in the Sales section. But what I will say is that if you have not listed all your products, (and most people forget just how many they have), and planned to market and sell more to your best customers you are missing out on SO MUCH instant cash and profits.

To eliminate the "I didn't know you did that" sin, I had one of my clients make a simple chart with products down one side and clients names along the top. The sales team then had the goal of getting each box in the grid ticked off – meaning they had spoken to every client about every product! This strategy gave them focus and made thousands of previously unforeseen profits.

So...what are you waiting for – get writing!

Give Your Customer or Prospect as Many Ways as Possible to Buy / Order from You

Often I see businesses that have slipped into the mindset of "how can we force the customer to buy from us in a way that makes it easy for us". WRONG!

We are all in business to serve our customers, in the words of the Blues Brothers – "You, Me – Everybody!" So why not give your customers as many different ways to pay as possible so you never give somebody the excuse not to order?

Client Case Study

One Internet retailing client of mine decided to test adding PayPal as a payment method to their already thriving site. The result was that 30% of customers decided to use it and sales jumped in just one month back to the levels of before the Credit Crunch! How much had they been missing just because people like the security or ease that PayPal gives them?

What other ways can you give your new and existing customers to buy from you?

- On-line / PayPal / Google Checkout, etc

- Fax Orders

- Order Phone Hotline

- Cheques by post

- Via sales people

- Debit Cards

- Credit Cards (remember to pass on the % fee so that your margins stay on track!)

- Staged payments via standing order or direct debit.

What two methods can you add to your business?

1 ....

2. ....

Invoice as Soon as You Can

So many businesses get caught up in selling and delivering that the task of invoicing gets relegated to the bottom of the administrative pile.

Start invoicing as soon as you can and the cash will flow faster.

Hold regular weekly or fortnightly invoice meetings to ensure good communication between sales and finance – if it's sold, invoice it NOW!

If you are delivering a project or service over a number of weeks or months ensure you set up a staged payment plan to help ease your cash flow. This is also a benefit to your client as it reassures them you'll finish the work.

Consider Selling off Any Old or Obsolete Stock, Vehicles or Office Furniture You No Longer Need

Let's be honest, most of us have old items we no longer use in our business that could generate some cash for us if we can sell them.

OK, this is not going to make you rich, I get that, but I have had clients with old capital equipment, vehicles or stock, etc., which they sold off to generate more cash to reinvest in Marketing to grow the business.

Take a moment to list items you could sell, even if you just used eBay to generate some quick cash.

Items I will sell off include:

....

....

Link Paying Sales Commissions to the Receipt of Payment Rather than Receipt of Order

This may not be the most popular strategy with your sales team, but it is the right one for the business right now.

There are three key cash flow benefits:

- You delay payment of the commission and keep your cash in the bank longer.

- Your sales people will be motivated to ensure their customers pay on time.

- Sales people will be less inclined to pressure-sell companies that may not be in a good financial position.

All of these help your business, which in turn helps their career.

Eliminate "Bleeding" Months

All businesses have their dead months when sales drop off for whatever reason and the businesses can be left carrying a significant loss. Many businesses I've coached have two or more months like this in any one year.

The key is to find alternative markets you can exploit with your existing products or services – or to find alternative, possibly joint ventures, products or services you can offer to your existing market in these months to at least get the business to break even, so that you stop the cash flowing OUT!

In some cases you can justify a seasonal special offer that is sold at cost, or just above, for that month only e.g. August, a renowned 'slow' month because of holidays, to generate enough cash to keep you moving.

Be careful, though, because unless framed up very precisely as to why you are discounting, your customers will expect this all the time.

Look into Invoice Factoring, or Cash Advances Against Sales as a Solution to Poor Cash Flow

Depending on the type of business you run and the strength of your clients, Government, NHS or Large Corporate, you may want to consider looking into factoring your invoices to free up cash, this is especially useful if large customers take over 90 days to pay!.

While this strategy will give you your cash faster, less than 7 days after invoice in some cases, it is important to understand that the Factor will deduct a commission and that if they can't collect the debt during the following 90 days they can and will ask for their money back! My advice is speak to your Bank manager and accountant and look at how good your current collection system is. If it's good you won't need this form of cash flow but it has helped a number of my fast-growth clients in the past. Lastly, be sure to check the terms and conditions of at least three Factoring companies before going ahead, and remember it's a negotiation – so never accept the first % price they quote..

Implement a Just-in-Time System to Reduce Your Stock Holdings

Today, most suppliers are quick to respond to an order and have fairly low minimum order quantities. Start working up a top 50 product list of best selling and highest margin products. These should be your never-run-out of items. Monitor how fast or slowly things are selling, and only order product you know you can move in small quantities.

Set a minimum stock level for each product. Base this on the average quantity you sell in a given time frame, (weekly or monthly etc.), and on the speed you can re-stock from your suppliers, this will take the guess work out of your stock levels.

Reduce Your Ranges / Focus on Top Sellers

This strategy requires the constant monitoring of sales on a week-by-week, month-by-month basis.

Thin out your product ranges and focus on the brands that people want and are still prepared to pay for. Less is more here and don't stock a new range until you have checked to see how many people search Google for it by name. If the numbers are low then the answer is NO – don't stock it.

Change Your Statement Layout

Don't send out statements that show an account is 30, 60, 90, 120 days overdue. This implies that it must be OK to wait 120 days to pay, after all, you have put a box there for it!

Review how your statements, look. Think of them as a marketing tool and the goal is to persuade them to pay you on time.

Client Story

One of my clients who sells to large Pharmaceutical companies prints his invoices on oversized pink paper. The people in the accounts department always wonder what it's for, even if it's on the bottom of a pile and as a result payment times have come down.

When you are sending out statements of overdue invoices, always include a copy of the original invoice. It will dramatically speed up payments as it makes life much easier for the customer.

Send a Chocolate "Thank You" with Your Invoices

This one is a bit of fun but also seems to work in speeding up payments.

It does harness the power of giving first and receiving after, – but either way you are likely to get your money faster!

Use Creative Customer Financing for New Projects

This is a great way to use your existing customers to help fund product development such as new software. An executive airline company recently got 200 of its customers to give a $100,000 non-refundable deposit down on a designer jet that had not even been made yet! Their deposits funded production and no need for bank finance.

How could you use this mindset or approach in your business, to create more working capital?

Get Tough with Non Payers

In my experience leopards don't change their spots and a Non Payer is a Non Payer is a Non Payer.

Now, if for some reason you did not pick this up early enough, it's time to take action – it's not personal, it's business.

If you have a debt you are unable to collect, call first, then send serious letters with final deadlines for payment. If this fails, hire a solicitor with a debt collection division and issue a court summons if you still cannot get satisfaction from them.

Yes, you may lose the customer, but do you want bad payers as customers?

Explain to your customer that you can, by law, charge compound interest on overdue invoices – tell them how much this would be and see them jump!

Client Case Study

I have a client who is a Solicitor and when people get very overdue (yes, even with solicitors) she sends them a letter informing them that she'll be reissuing their invoice, with the new compounding interest included if the old bill is not settled in 5 days. So far she has a 100% success rate at getting these late payers to pay!

Consider Setting Up a Staged Payment Plan for Very Overdue Debts

Some money is better than no money, so if you have long term debtors – get them onto a regular payment plan and insist on a standing order or direct debit arrangement.

You may have to wait 12 months to get it all, but at least it will start flowing now.

It also shows you are willing to support and work with your customers through difficult times, which they will appreciate when times get better.

Turn Dead Stock Into Cash

If you are holding old stock or last season's stock
GET REAL and realise that its value is only ever
going to go down the longer you hold onto it, so
sell it – NOW.

Here are some ways to create a buzz clearing it:

- A by-invitation private sale to past customers

- A "Fire" sale with burning offers up to 75% off

- A 'one day only, everything must go' event

- Get a local celebrity to help promote it

- Give a percentage to charity and tell the press to raise awareness
  (plus it's good to give back to others)

However you decided to market it just GET IT SOLD!

Negotiate Spread Payment Terms With Your Suppliers

This may seem like a very obvious strategy, but you would be amazed
how many businesses do not undertake this as a matter of course.

What suppliers want right now is a commitment that you'll still use
them so they can plan. So in exchange for offering them this
support, negotiate better prices but also longer payment terms.

Once you agree these be sure to stick to them and pay on the agreed
dates. We all need our suppliers and without them and their good
will we can't serve our customers.

Remember: treat your suppliers as you would like to be treated and
you can't go wrong.

Use Creative Personal Financing if Needed

Before you start thinking I am suggesting strange accounting practices, or MP-like expense claims, wait just a moment. Yes credit may not be as readily available on every street corner as it was, but there are still good deals to be had.

You must "think outside the Bank" at times like these. Here are a few I've leveraged in the past...

I have used interest free credit cards at times to fund purchases where cash was tight in my business, and then paid it off over the 9 month period. I've bartered services or supplies with customers to reduce the cash pressure when needed, and I've even sold off unwanted office furniture on e-bay.

List 2 creative finance options you have access to:

1 ....

....

....

2. ....

....

....

Action Steps:

Now take a moment to list the top three strategies from this chapter you will implement.

1 ....

....

....

....

2. ....

....

....

....

3. ....

....

....

....

If you have any questions on this chapter...

Go to **www.AskPaulAvins.com** and ask me!

"Profit is one of the key ways you
keep score in a business."

Chapter 7:

Profit Margins

"The language of business is accounting."

— Warren Buffet, Investor

"If you don't understand the language, you can't play the game!"

— Keith Cunningham, Finance and Business Speaker

No Dirt Here... Just Gold!

Let's just get something clear before we get into the proven profit-building strategies, and it's this...

Profit is NOT a dirty word!

In my experience, too many speakers at wealth creation seminars, make owners almost feel guilty if they make large profits, which in turn means they limit their business growth or sabotage what's working without even knowing why.

It's as though they have a belief that making money will turn them into a bad person!

The reality is that, if you are in business, your obligation to the company, yourself, your customers, your team and your suppliers is to make a profit. If you don't, everybody on this list stands to lose out!

As the Author of the 1 Minute Entrepreneur Ken Blanchard puts it:

> *"Profit is the applause you get for taking care of customers and creating a motivating environment for your people..."*
>
> — Ken Blanchard

With all the negativity in the media right now you could be forgiven for thinking that the only way to achieve this is through cost-cutting on a massive scale.

In a few cases this may be necessary, and, if you have to do this, do it fast, do enough of it, and get it over so you can move forward. In reality, though, most businesses can only go so far in cutting costs before they start impeding the ability of the business to deliver to its customers.

So the real answer is that you have to cut and manage your costs, but you also have to focus on GROWING your sales. In my experience there are not many problems in a business that can't be improved or solved by a major boost in sales!

I've listed here a few of the key sales strategies that give you a quick boost in profits, but I suggest you study the sections on Sales and Marketing as well, if you have jumped straight to this page.

Client Case Study

"Since working with Paul my Profit margins are up 87%. They just don't teach you these strategies in Business School!"

— Mike Chilman (MD), MCFP Ltd

Create a "Financial Dashboard" to Give You Real Time Feedback on What is Happening

If you don't have a 'financial dashboard' in your business, how can you ever hope to drive your business from Surviving to Thriving?

This is the foundation which enables everything else to function.

There are some fundamentals that every business owner needs to be looking at, as well as some that will be specific to your industry.

Here's what I coach my clients to have as a minimum:

- Monthly Profit and Loss within 7-10 days of the end of month

- 6-8 week rolling Cash Flow forecast

- Monthly Balance Sheet – this tells you the current value of your business

- Weekly Debtors and Creditors lists

- Weekly Cash in the bank

- VAT, National Insurance or Corporation Tax liability

- Average Order Value

- Gross and Net % Profit Per Sale

- Turnover & Profit per employee

If you are a retailer you'll also want to consider stock turn, or turnover per square foot as well.

Make Sure You have a Budget for Profit

The scary fact is that most business owners I work with, don't have a written budget they are actively working towards when I start coaching them. A few do, of course, but most people at best only have a number they are shooting for in their head, but no system for monitoring and checking how they are doing.

If you want to thrive and profit in this recession you have to have a documented budget. I coach my clients to start with the amount of Net Profit they want to make then work backwards, factoring in all the fixed costs etc. This will then give you a clear idea of what your sales need to be to deliver this with your current cost structure.

This may show that your cost base is too high and needs cutting, or that you need to invest more in marketing if you are to hit your sales targets.

Two key points to remember:

• If you don't have a budget then getting monthly Profit & Loss figures and a Balance sheet will not help you as much, because you have nothing to compare your actual performance against.

• Make sure you put your salary in the budget forecast. Too many business owners say, "I'll take what's left at the end of each month", rather than insisting the business makes enough to pay them what they need or want.

You should always get paid first, every month, not after your suppliers. This will create positive pressure on you to generate sales, as well as improving your personal cash flow!

Reduce Costs by As Much As Possible

Time to get serious – you'll need to cut costs and drive efficiency to thrive right now so take time out to look at everything.

Set a goal to reduce your operating expenses then re-negotiate everything you currently buy.

Here are a few areas in which quick wins can be gained:

- Rent reduction, as no landlord wants to lose a tenant right now

- Mobile phone charges – lots of great offers and new tariffs out there

- Insurance is a great one to shop around for

- Stationery is a commodity, so consider buying own brand vs major brand as you can save over 10% on this alone

- Move to electronic invoicing and banking to cut postage and bank charges

- Move your team onto a 4-day week or reduce their basic salary, but offer profit-sharing or commissions so you pay more for results

- Vehicle leasing contracts – prices have fallen by over 25% compared to this time last year

Stop Non-performing Marketing Activities

There is more on this in the Marketing section, but essentially this strategy is all about knowing what's really working in your business and stopping what's not.

The old saying that "50% of my advertising is working but I don't know which 50%" is just rubbish, as all marketing activities can have their performance monitored and tracked. Then stop under-performing marketing and put the money back in your bank account, or into marketing activities that are working.

Up-Sell and Cross-Sell More

There is more on this in the Sales section but a key point to remember here, is that it's a lot more PROFITABLE to sell to your existing customers than it is to go out and get new ones.

The easiest way to do this is to cross-sell or link up-sell. Recent on-line tests have shown that over 50% of customers will take advantage of a relevant up-sell offer, at the time of purchase, if it's not more that 60% of the price of the first item they were buying.

I bet you, like me, have been sold additional books by Amazon who made a point of telling you that people who had purchased the book you'd just ordered, also bought these other books.

Yes, this is very simple, and you may already be doing it, but are you doing it in a systematic way to every customer every time?

If not – start today!

Client Story

I have a coaching client who created a Profit Matrix™ so she could see what products and services her clients were purchasing and which were left to see to. Then every day for 30 mins she sends e-mails to clients telling them about things they don't yet buy from her. Her record is £7,000 in new sales in 30 mins!

What could you up-sell and cross-sell to your existing customers starting today?

....

....

....

....

....

....

Make Sure NO One Customer Represents More than a Maximum of 20% of Your Turnover or Profit

Too often when we start working with a big customer we get very excited about the growth potential, and really give them a lot of attention, and rightly so. However, the danger is we get so focused on looking after them that we stop going after more new business, and wake up one day to find they have become more than 40% of our total turnover. Make sure you don't let any one client represent more than 20% of your turnover and always be asking yourself the question: if they went bust on us or took their business to our competition, could we survive?

If the answer is NO, start working on fixing this today!

Deliver Products or Services that have an Ongoing Revenue Attached / Turn 1 Sale into Many Sales

This is a very powerful way to boost your bottom line and one that, with a little thought, any business can take advantage of. It's important to remember that the payments don't just have to be monthly, as in many cases, they can be weekly, quarterly or even annually. The critical point is that you set customers up with an "until further notice" option, where they keep paying you until they cancel. Here are three examples of businesses that use this very effectively:

- Gym memberships

- Magazine and Internet Subscriptions

- Annual maintenance contracts for photocopiers etc

If you can create a "Members Club" your customers can join as well this will further lock in their loyalties and increase your profits.

Have an Automated Pricing Model that Forces your Sales People to Sell Above a Minimum Margin

Too often in my experience sales people really don't understand the negative impact they can have on your business's Net Margin, by giving away what they perceive to be small top line discounts to win the business.

Example:

Product sells for £100 – Costs of £80 = Profit of £20

Salesperson gives 10% discount / £100 x 10% = £10

Profit of £20 - £10 discount = 50% reduction in Your Profit!

A simple way to stop this happening is to force your sales people to use an electronic pricing tool that fixes the minimum margin they can make.

Client Case Study

One of my clients recently discovered that adding just £50 per £1,000 on every quote, would have resulted in a net profit increase of nearly £350,000 in the previous 12-months. More than a 125% increase! When he implemented this there was NO impact on conversion rate.

STOP Discounting and Offer High Perceived Value Products Instead

Giving away top line discounts can have a disastrous effect on your profits, as we have already proved in the last strategy. The reality is that you'll be up against businesses who do offer discounts and this is how you compete. Rather than offering discounts – offer products or services that have a high perceived value (RRPs – Recommended Retail Price) but a low cost in real terms to the business.

Here are some examples of the type of things clients of mine have offered:

- Extended guarantees

- Free upgrades

- Free maintenance visits

- Bonus products that suppliers wanted to clear out

- Vouchers for complimentary products or services (you can do this as a marketing exercise with another company to help them generate leads)

- Free Memberships

One important point to remember is that you MUST tell people what the full price of the bonus or free gift would normally be, or they don't appreciate the value and the strategy doesn't deliver the maximum impact.

Stop Under-Charging. Price at What You Are REALLY Worth

The fastest way to go bust right now is to UNDER charge and OVER deliver. Both of which are activities that are driven by a fear of loss. Loss of business, loss of customers, loss of sales – but the reality is 180° away from this illusion.

If you have a clear USP (see Sales section) and are clearly adding value to your clients you can increase your price even in the current market.

5 Quick Client Stories to illustrate my point

- An accounting and bookkeeping firm in my Wealth Club recently increased their prices by more than 10% and actually won more business!

- A children's nursery coaching client of mine has increased prices by 3% for the next year and they are over-subscribed and have a waiting list.

- A martial arts centre I coach put up their prices at the end of 2008 and has seen membership grow by 35%.

- A drycleaners increased prices by 15% and it had no impact on sales so this extra money went straight to the bottom line

- A web design company put their prices up 30% in the last 6 months and their conversion rate has stayed exactly the same – WOW!

Price is often viewed as an indicator of quality, especially in the service business sector. Go back and price check your competition then review your own prices. I'll bet there are areas you can increase which will deliver profits straight to the bottom line.

Commit to start testing higher prices in your business today and get paid what you are really worth.

Use Bundles of Complimentary Products

I recently took my 3-year-old son to a bike shop to get his first bike. It really struck me that once I had bought the bike nobody in the shop offered me any other products!

What would have happened if they had offered me a *First Bike Starter Pack* which included a bell, helmet, gloves, knee pads, 12-month bike insurance against theft, etc?

I would more than likely have taken it as they are the experts and this must be what I need. It would have boosted their average order value and their profit margins – a great result for very little extra effort.

What could you package together for your prospects and customers?

Make Sure You Are Charging For Everything

I have seen good businesses literally give away thousands of pounds in profits by not paying attention to this one area.

Here are just a few things businesses forget to charge for:

- Delivery or urgent next day delivery

- Credit Card Charges

- Changes to specifications after the order is placed which generate more work not priced for

- Extra design time if the brief is changed by the customer

> **Go back and look at your business to see what else you should and could be charging for then list them below:**
>
> ....
>
> ....
>
> ....
>
> ....
>
> ....
>
> ....
>
> ....

Implement Sales Bonuses Based on Hitting Profit Targets

Having sales targets based on turnover is a disaster waiting to happen, sales people will do whatever they can to earn commission and if they aren't focused on margin then discounts will bring pain to your life as a business owner.

Set a minimum level of margin contribution (Gross) they have to deliver every month BEFORE they start to earn their commission. This should recover their costs, including things such as car and fuel. The more you teach your sales force the difference between turnover and profit the better. And you won't have to work so hard!

TIP: Implement pricing software (or Excel spreadsheets) that ensures a minimum margin is always quoted. Anything below this needs higher authority sign-off.

Review Your Terms & Conditions

This strategy is in the Profits section because if you are incurring overdraft charges because of poor cash flow, then it's a direct hit on your bottom line as you are, in effect, becoming your customers' banker!

There is no law that says you must operate 30-day payment terms – you make the rules you want to play by so that you have control.

Your new customers will go with whatever your terms are, because they don't know any different, so why not change them to work for you and your bottom line?

How you do it can depend on the type of business you operate:

Service Business:

- Ask for money on account

- Set up a standing order to ensure regular cash flow

- Ask for cash up front

Product Business:

- Implement a staged payment process when milestones are hit

- Cash with order

- Payment on delivery

The reason people don't do this is a fear they will lose the business – you won't. Only the poor payers will walk away and you didn't want them anyway.

Shop Around and Get at Least Three Quotes for Significant Purchases

All too often we get comfortable with a supplier we've used for years, and it may be some time since you price checked them against the competition.

Make it a rule going forward to always get three quotes, one from your existing supplier and two from the competition. If they beat your existing price you have power to negotiate with. If you're existing supplier was still the best value you can sleep well that night.

Allow Purchasing ONLY With a PO (Purchase Order)

The idea of delegating the ability for people in your business to purchase what they need sounds great, but if there are no checks and balances to monitor it – you'll just end up bleeding profits.

Make sure that to runalong side your budgets you have a Purchase Order System that means people can't buy something unless it's approved by a manager or by you. This has saved clients of mine tens of thousands of pounds, and stops your team buying anything on impulse, which can lead to too much poor-selling stock or avalanches of stationery clogging up your office.

For extra power, tie this in with a profit share to your team, and watch how they start seeing ways to get by with what they have!

Join a Buying Group or Business Organisation

This can be a very quick and easy win for you. In most industries there is some type of buying group that you can join, where members can club together to have more buying power with the suppliers they all deal with on a regular basis.

If there isn't one in your area or industry, why not consider starting one?

Alternatively, if you join business organisations such as the Chamber of Commerce or the Federation of Small Businesses, you'll get discounts on everything from insurance to mobile phone calls.

Buy ONLY What You Need

All too often we just go through the motions of buying what we think we need and really go for the what-would-be-nice-to-haves.

STOP – ask yourself "Do I really need to make this purchase to move the business forward?"

Consider trading services with a supplier rather than spending cash, or just place the minimum you can order and then order often. This will also have a positive impact on your cash flow.

Conduct Frequent Stock-takes

If you hold stock either in your shop or warehouse this is a MUST. Most people leave this until the end of the year, which just makes the task worse and gives you no management information to work from during the previous 12-months.

In today's climate you should stock-take at least every 90 days, and, ideally, every month. This will show you where you have slow moving product lines, which you can then push with a sale or special offer, to generate cash and reinvest in faster moving lines.

Every 90 days look at your bottom 20% and clear out. The faster you turn your stock the more profit you make at the end of the year.

Eliminate Duplication

So much money is wasted today in businesses with poor processes and systems. Often simple things like entering the customer's contact details, may have to be done in two or three different pieces of software – e.g. Order System, Accounting System and Dispatch System, to name just a few.

Use the time now to look at removing duplication and inefficiency in your business. You may need to upgrade or invest in new technology to make this happen, but it'll deliver results in profit and morale to your team.

What areas of duplication do you need to remove?

....

....

....

....

....

....

....

Claim Government Grants

Right now there are many Government Grants and training initiatives available to businesses to help them get through this recession.

These do vary depending on your geographical location and the size of business, of course, but could save you money on things you were already budgeting to invest in.

For example, right now there is a Directors' Development fund that small and medium sized businesses can apply for with up to £1,100 towards Coaching and Mentoring. For more info on this contact your local Business Link Advisor.

Claim this and use it to work with me on growing your business!

Boost Your Team's Productivity

When economic conditions tighten up you need to get as much as possible out of your resources, and the main resource for most businesses is its people.

Understanding this technique has really helped my clients see where they were wasting time, but more importantly where their teams were wasting time – in some cases as much as 40% of their week – up to 16 hours a week per person!

Here's what you do. Have EVERYBODY in your business, including you, fill in a time audit for a week. This is in 20 minute chunks so 3 sections per hour where you log what you've been doing – everybody must agree to be 100% honest in this. It helps if you, as the owner, say you'll share yours with the team so everybody is being held accountable.

This will create some pressure for people who are not performing, and they may push back and create a fuss. Carry on anyway, as the information will enable you to manage your most important investment to give you a higher return.

Stop Paying Overtime or Reduce Hours

This may not be a popular strategy with the team but it forces them to become more focused and productive. The reality is that most people let their work fill the time available, so if they know they get paid for running over they run over. If they have to get it finished by 5 p.m. or they work for free, they'll get it done 95% of the time.

If you are really feeling the "crunch" you may have to put people on 4 day weeks as it's cheaper in the long run to keep a team intact if you can, than to re-recruit when times pick up, as they will eventually.

Reduce your Creditor Days

If you have a poor credit control procedure in place then you are being a bank to your customers and I'll bet you're not charging them for it!

This is a CRITICAL number you should be monitoring on a regular basis. Set a goal for your debtor days – less that 30 days etc.

Look at your invoicing documents to make sure they are clear and correct so the customer has no excuse for delaying payment.

I see some companies that issue statement with boxes at the bottom of 30, 60, 90, 120 days with the customer's overdue balance in the appropriate box. I understand what they are trying to do, but what they are communicating, in fact, is that it's OK to take up to 120 days to pay your bill as we've put a box for it on your invoice!

Next, if people take 60 days to pay a 30 day invoice, change your terms to 7 days so you start chasing it sooner – then you may get it in 30 days.

Top Tip: Send out your invoices on bright colour paper, it will get noticed and paid faster.

Cut your Credit Card Charges

If you take credit cards, this simple little script will help you move people across to debit cards or cash.

Here's what you do:

When they come to pay, simply ask them if they would prefer to pay Debit Card or Cash? This saves you the credit card charges and most people will take the debit card option if they are not carrying cash.

Thanks to Paul Fowler from Enstone Flying club who perfected this, and shared it with me and our members at a Wealth Club meeting.

Outsource for a Fixed Price where Possible

To keep your people overhead low but still have skill and creativity availability, outsourcing can be a great resource. If you employ subcontractors, putting them on a fixed price for the job vs a day rate ensures that you manage your cost base, and the subcontractor has a reason to be more productive to get onto the next job so he can earn more money.

Never outsource on a time and materials basis. Always get a budget and always agree a fixed price, with penalties on late delivery if appropriate.

Action Steps:

Now take a moment to list the top three strategies from this chapter you will implement.

1 ....

....

....

....

2. ....

....

....

....

3. ....

....

....

....

If you have any questions on this chapter...

Go to **www.AskPaulAvins.com** and ask me!

Chapter 8:

Team

> *"In Sports the best teams have the best coaches and I believe the same should be true in business. Working with Paul has really paid off for us."*
>
> — MD Chris Lewis, Chris Lewis Fire and Security (coaching client for over 6 years)

Your People are Your Biggest Asset

In business, nobody succeeds on their own – it's that simple. But as your business goes through different stages it will require different people with differing skills and abilities.

As a leader you need to know how to attract, keep, motivate and grow your biggest asset – your people...

Great businesses have great visions but without great people, and great systems for these people to implement – all the good intentions can be lost.

In this section I've pulled together some of the critical strategies my clients are using today to build high-performing teams even in today's more challenging climate.

In some cases, you may need to restructure before you can move forward. If that's the case, act quickly, as one negative person can drag a business down. It's important to remember this is a never-ending process. People will always come and go in your business but as long as you have the *Talent Recruitment and Development Strategy* you'll have access to the right people at the right time.

Be Honest and Open about the Businesses Performance

Tell them the TRUTH.

If your team is to pull together and help your business not only survive but to thrive during this current recession, then they need to know the reality of your situation.

Don't let your own FEAR stop you from sharing. Remember that it's just:

F – False

E – Emotions

A – Appearing

R – Real

Your people are not blind – they know what's happening in the world – and they will want to help, but you have to let them know how.

If the truth scares them off they were never really on your team anyway!

Share your Personal Pain so they Realise that You are All in this Together

Often, employees have this false perception that THEY are the only ones feeling any pain, especially if you are in the process of implementing pay cuts or redundancies.

If you have had to take a personal pay cut, or even stop paying yourself for a few months to help the business, then tell them. One, it will help them with their pain, two, it will demonstrate true leadership and three, it will show them you are all in the same boat.

Teams like leaders who are human and vulnerable as well as strong and driven.

Show the Numbers on a Flip Chart or White Board

This is simple but VERY powerful.

If you don't already you should have the monthly or weekly sales figures displayed, so everybody can see where you are. At times this may not be pleasant for everybody, but at least people will feel included and often they will have ideas to help with sales.

You'll be amazed how much people focus on them towards the end of a month to see what else they can do to hit the target. After all what's the point in playing the game if you don't know the score, or how long is left to play?

Create a Culture of Accountability

I can't emphasise just how important it is to create a Culture of Accountability in your business. Too often, as business owners, we let people get away with not doing what they commit to, or, worse, we decide to jump in and do it ourselves to save time!

A recent survey found that employees were working at an average of less than 45% of their capacity! Wow! How much money is that costing companies just like yours every year?

Remember: PRODUCTIVITY = PROFITABILITY

Implement a one-week time audit monitoring what everybody is doing every 20 minutes... including you! This will be met by resistance as nobody likes to be under this type of scrutiny, but it will show you where tasks are being duplicated and just how much time is being wasted - and where to implement changes.

Hold More Regular, Structured Team Meetings

In difficult times you need to communicate more with your team, not less. It's easy to just focus on *doing* and *activity* when, in reality, communication will be key to your survival and success.

Hold weekly team meetings, even if they are just 30 minute updates and shares. It's important to start with the Wins people have had from the previous week, however small they were. In these troubled times it's important to keep reminding everyone what good things are still in the business.

Review sales opportunities and ideas. Monitor costs and set weekly goals so everybody is clear on how they can help.

It's critical to get 100% inclusion, so if you have part- timers, work with them so they get included.

Put Your Best People to Work on Your Best Opportunities

How often do we let our best people end up fire- fighting during tough times? Too often,I would suggest. Right now you need to be looking for the next opportunity in your market because there will be one and it will arrive. Will you be ready for it?

Use your resources to balance the need for short-term revenue and medium-term opportunities.

Giving your best people a brightness of future is essential, if you are to keep them motivated and on your team, as they are the last people you want to lose.

Remember: the 80/20 rule. 80% of your future results will come from just 20% of your opportunities. Make sure your top people are working on these now.

List the top opportunity in your business right now:

....

....

....

....

Who is working on this?

....

....

....

Who should be working on this / as well?

....

....

....

Implement a Bonus Scheme Based on Hitting Gross Profit Targets

When I coach clients, one of the most frequently asked questions I get around teams is "How do I reward the team and not just for Sales, for results?"

The critical number you want them to be driving for here is your Gross Profit Target per month. It should be front and centre for everybody, as it will move them into *Ownership Thinking* which is treating your money like it's their own.

After all, making a consistent profit is a team effort – it keeps the business stable and your team employed!

Remember: the bonus you may pay out does not always have to be cash, it could be a team night out, a Pizza lunch in the office on a Friday or whatever would motivate your people.

In my experience, if you build an element of FUN into these, they work better and the positive impact lasts longer.

Strip Out the "Deadwood"

There is no getting away from it, people are usually the biggest overhead in a business and, when sales decline, cuts have to be made.

It's vitally important that you follow the proper HR procedures but for now stop and ask yourself this question:

If you had to go back and rehire your team based on what you now know about them...who would you not take back and why?

Answering this will give you a great place to start working from.

If you need specific HR help contact Heather Salter from Jigsaw HR **www.jigsawHR.co.uk** She is a Wealth Club member and fantastic at what she does.

Cross-Training People for Productivity

If people are a fixed cost then you must look at how to get a greater return on them as an asset. After all, if they were a machine you would want them running at full speed for as many hours as possible.

One way to do this is to look at cross-training them to undertake more than a one job role. When times are tough, this can add huge value to the business and reduce costs. It can also raise morale, as almost everybody would rather be doing something useful, than be sitting around feeling useless.

Client Case Study

I have a coaching client who owns a Coach Travel business. When a driver is not actually driving he is sitting in the bus costing money and doing nothing to help the business (except secure the bus, of course). Sometimes this is for up to 8 hours. My client needed a new web site, so he asked if any of his drivers were interested in learning how to develop a web site. Now he has a driver with his own laptop, a 3G card, a new web site built and managed for no additional labour costs, and a new site generating business in just 3 days after it launched!

Use Personality Profiles to Boost Performance

The sad fact is that often businesses don't really understand how their people are wired inside. What motivates them, frustrates them, what role they are best suited to and in which role they will find it almost impossible to be successful.

Right now you need the right people in the right roles, so get them profiled.

We use the Flippen Profile tool (for more info visit the **paul-avins.com** web site), but there are others such as DiSC or PeopleClues™. When your team understand themselves more you will get an increase in performance. When you understand how to manage them you will get an increase in performance. Combine these with each member of the team being in the right role and the sky is the limit!

Special Offer: Buy 2 Flippen Development Profiles for your team members and get a third FREE valued at £295. All profiles come with a 1-hour coaching session!

Keep it FUN

As one of my mentors once said to me, "if you take business too seriously it will kill you!"

OK, that may not be strictly true, but it does make a point.

Yes, I understand that currently things are not easy, so it's our responsibility as business leaders to ensure we create as much Fun as possible. After all, when we are having fun we sell better, serve our customers better, get along with our team members better and so are more productive.

There is enough negative news out there – make a decision to make your business a No Negative Zone. Focus on what is working, however small the wins are, and start enjoying the process of learning to thrive. After all, we are going to be in this economic mess for a while yet, so we might as well decide to make the best of it.

What 3 things can you start doing to put the fun back into your business?

1 ....

....

....

....

2. ....

....

....

....

3. ....

....

....

....

Build a Power Network of Support

Whatever business you are in you are going to need to have great people around you. One of the critical teams to build is your Business Power Team™ (BPT)

Here are a few of the key people I think you should have access to on your **BPT (Business Power Team)**:

- Business Coach

- Commercial Lawyer

- Accountant

- Tax Advisor

- Business Banker

- Financial Advisor

You'll find quotes and offers from many of my Wealth Club members at the back of this book.

Include your Suppliers on Your Team

At my seminars people often say to me, "I don't have a team, there are just two of us" or "We are just starting up. How does this work on team apply to me?"

Great questions, but I always suggest that they think of their team as not only people they employ, but also the people they use as suppliers.

This simple shift in focus can change the whole way you view the relationships and the results you get.

Consider bringing all your key suppliers together for a day. Share your vision and plans, ask about theirs and discuss ways you can help each other to succeed in the future.

Before you know it you'll have created your own Business Power Team.

Set up a Recruitment System

With the current costs of a wrong hire and replacement averaging out at over £100,000 when you include management time and lost opportunity costs, this is an area that deserves more attention than it gets in most companies.

Here are a few top tips from my Speed Recruitment System™:

• Create a nice-to-have versus a must-have list against which you can review the CVs you get.

• Conduct first stage interviews over the phone.

• Always interview at least 3 people for the role.

• Create interview check lists.

• Have different people interview the candidates in different locations to see how they adapt and interact with your existing team.

• Use Profiling tools where appropriate (e.g. Flippen).

• ALWAYS check their references before they start working for you.

• Conduct exit interviews before people leave so you can learn how to improve their role.

Hold Regular Team Appraisals

For some, the word *appraisal* generates fear and dread, as in corporate life they can be a very negative experience.

My suggestion is to call them *feedback sessions* where your team members get to learn what they are doing well. Critical to start with is, what areas they can focus on to get even better, no more than three in any one period between reviews.

It should also be an opportunity for your team member to ask for help, support and training to enable them to achieve their goals for the business.

Action Steps:

Now take a moment to list the top three strategies from this chapter you will implement.

1 ....

....

....

....

2. ....

....

....

....

3. ....

....

....

....

If you have any questions on this chapter...

Go to **www.AskPaulAvins.com** and ask me!

"Time is our most valuable asset,
yet we tend to waste it, kill it, and
spend it rather than invest it"
— Jim Rohn

Chapter 9:

Time

> *"You don't need to get*
> *ship-wrecked to get everything done by Friday!"*
>
> — Paul Avins

Making the Most of this Irreplaceable Asset

Time, the great leveller. It does not matter what size of business we run, what we do for a living or how much money we have, we all only have 1440 minutes (24 hours) in a day. These expire at the end of the day, you can't cash them in or hold them over. Then one day you will be out of credit and there is no overdraft facility at this bank!

The reality is we all waste a huge amount of time every day. Some things we do are positive activities but some, such as watching TV, are not.

This is an area of my life that is a constant battle for me because, although I am very driven, staying focused and finishing a project without getting distracted by the next exciting project is hard.

I've read countless books on time management, listened to lots of CDs and even taken courses on it. The fact is that none of us can manage time – we can only manage ourselves. And as Lao Tsu once said, "He who conquers others is strong. He who conquers himself is mighty."

Here are a few of the ideas and strategies that have helped me over the years. I hope they help you as well.

Set Compelling Goals

The Bible says, "Without a vision, the people perish" and I can tell you, from first-hand experience, a clear and compelling vision can extend your life by years as well as keep you focused and disciplined.

Here is my alternative take on the SMART formula of goal setting. As you are writing down your list of goals, make sure that each one is:

S – Specific

M – Motivational

A – Actionable (is there a next step?)

R – Relevant (to your bigger vision)

T – Trackable (who's holding you accountable?)

Do the Worst Relevant Task First

I am a big fan of Brian Tracy and I love his book *Eat That Frog* – it's a real masterpiece.

For me, the most powerful strategy in it is to do the worst thing on your list first, as this just gives you a huge sense of achievement and positive energy, that carries into the rest of your day.

Brian calls this 'eating a frog'. After all, when you've got that bad thing out of the way – the rest of your day can't help but taste sweeter, right? Be sure to check that eating this frog gets you closer to your medium-to-long-term goals, and is not just firefighting, or you'll struggle to move forward at the speed you desire.

Work on Your No.1 Goal First

Take a moment to look at your top 10 goals in your business for this year. If you don't have a list like this then STOP and write one out right now!

OK.... now look at your list and select the one that, if you could achieve it in the next 7 days, would have the biggest positive impact on your business.

There is usually one that jumps out for people when I do this exercise at my seminars.

Now your job is to spend the first hour of every day working towards the achievement of this goal. Do this before you turn on your BlackBerry or check your e-mail or Twitter account.

By doing this you'll bring the Law of Compounding into play and achieve more than you can possibly imagine.

Go on Holiday More Often

I bet this one got your attention!

Have you ever noticed just how much you get done the week before you go away on holiday? It's just amazing what a real, compelling deadline can do for your focus and discipline.

What would be the impact if you took more holidays in a year, not less?

I coach my clients to get away every 90 days, even if it's just for a long weekend. It not only forces them to be more productive, it also gives them head space to think and come up with new ideas. When they come back to their businesses they have renewed energy, passion and ideas to drive forward.

Schedule in Relax and Disconnect Time

Client Story

At one of my seminars I asked a room of Property Investors when they had their most profitable ideas? One man said he got a £1 million idea when he went on holiday! I asked him how often he went away? He said just once a year as he could not afford the time! I asked him how many £1 million ideas would he have if he took 4 holidays a year? He got the point and committed to take a holiday every 90 days for the rest of the year.

So, how many times a year do you want to go away?

I know this can sound like a contradiction, but, as business owners and entrepreneurs we can become so caught up in our latest project or idea, that we work all the available hours we have.

It's vital, in my view, that you plan in downtime, or time with the family. Just because you can be connected to your office 24/7 doesn't mean you should be.

Log off the Internet, turn off your mobile and give yourself the gift of time to do what you want.

As one of my mentors said to me: "Kids spell Love "T.I.M.E" and I would say the same goes for your relationships and health as well.

Implement Time Blocking

So many of us let other people control our diary when in reality, if we thought about it, we could massively increase our productivity by blocking out chunks of our diary for key activities.

Of course to do this you need to be clear what your key activities are. Here are a few suggestions that have really helped my clients over the years:

- Have a Marketing Monday at least once a month, just to work on your marketing

- Regular Finance Friday meetings

- Monthly Team meetings

- Weekly or monthly Sales meeting

- Supplier days when you see all your suppliers' sales people back to back rather than throughout the week

- Strategic Time – planning for future growth

- Personal Development & Learning time

However you do it, make a commitment to get back control of your diary today!

Use Technology to Leverage Time

The greater your productivity, the greater your profitability. As the old saying goes ... "Time is Money."

Think about ways to use technology to do more with less effort, less travelling and less stress. Use conference calls, GoToMeeting.com, file sharing, intranets, extranets etc.

I have clients who have seen an increase in their sales peoples productivity, and orders when they use a BlackBerry.

Turn Dead Time into Wealth Time

There is a direct link between the relevant knowledge which you both have and implement, and the level of your success in the market place. This has been a guiding principle in my whole business life.

Start today investing in YOU. It's the best investment you'll ever make.

• Read Books

• Listen to CDs in your car or on an iPod at the gym

• Watch Educational DVDs

• Attend Seminars

• Get a Coach

Key Point: If you think education is expensive, try ignorance!

Have Agendas and End Times for all Meetings

How many times have you called or gone into a meeting that has dragged on and on, wasting everybody's time?

Get control back by always having an agenda, even if it is just three key points you want to cover in a short 15 minute meeting.

Have a start time and a finish time that everybody is aware of and stick to it. You'll be amazed at how much more focused and energized everybody will be.

Entertainment vs Education Ratio

Successful people in all walks of life invest in themselves. One of my mentors told me when I was just in my twenties to:

"Invest 10% of everything you earn back into learning and growing your skills."

I'll take credit for being smart enough to do what he suggested and I encourage you to do the same.

Take a look at how much you invest in your Entertainment versus your Education. I bet you'll find you are spending more on fun than on learning – and the results you are getting prove it.

Investing just 20 minutes a day - every day in learning new skills can transform your sales, cash flow, profits, team, health, relationships and wealth.

If you can't commit to this, are you really serious about your success? To learn from some of the best teachers in the world on a daily basis visit **www.learntogrowyourbusiness.tv**

Get Enough Sleep

Tiredness makes cowards of us all. Not only that, it affects our ability to make good judgment and that, in business, can cost you dearly.

Research shows we need 6-8 hours sleep on a regular basis.
Yes, we can live with less, and on many occasions I have, but you can't sustain it over the long term.

So – get to bed earlier!

Make sure you keep a note pad by your bed as when you wake up refreshed and with good ideas you'll want to capture them before they slip away.

Plan for Tomorrow Before Finishing Today

This is very simple, but that does not make it easy. Never finish your working day without planning your top goals or actions for the following day.

This allows your subconscious mind to work on them while you sleep – more leverage – and you'll wake up focused and ready to go, so you hit the ground running.

Implementing this in your life will save you hours per week which will compound over the years into thousands of pounds in additional profits.

Get a Coach who will Hold You Accountable

The best thing about working for yourself is:

• You don't have a boss!

The worst thing about working for yourself is:

• You don't have a boss!

So the only person who knows if you put off critical actions or avoid tough decisions is YOU. Doing this slows down your success and will have a negative impact on your self-belief and self-image.

I have coached over 150 business owners including 15 millionaires, and a lot of them knew what to do but they just never got around to it – sound familiar?

When you hire a business coach, they will drive you to do the 20% that will deliver you 80% of your results. Just imagine what that would mean to your bottom line!! I have been blessed with the coaches in my life, business life and health and as Tiger Woods once said:

"No matter how tough you are, nobody succeeds on their own."

Want to have me coach you or your sales team? Send me an e-mail at **success@paul-avins.com** and I'll send you an application form.

To watch videos of some of my client's results visit **www.paul-avins.com**

15 Minutes for Money

This strategy is fun and profitable at the same time. Simply set a reminder in your diary every day when you'll stop whatever you are doing and focus on making or saving money for the next 15 minutes.

Now this may include:

• Calling a past customer to see if they need anything else

• Cancelling an unused subscription

• Chasing up an overdue debt

• Following up a refund you're due

• Shopping around on-line for quotes for commodity products

Whatever you do you must do something EVERY day for the compounding element of this to work though. When you do, you'll be having more fun and making more money, a real win-win in my book.

Action Steps:

Now take a moment to list the top three strategies from this chapter you will implement.

1 ....

....

....

....

2. ....

....

....

....

3. ....

....

....

....

If you have any questions on this chapter...

Go to **www.AskPaulAvins.com** and ask me!

"If you don't know which
destination you're sailing to,
no wind is favorable."

Chapter 10:

Implementing Your SOS Success Plan

You have to start right NOW!

The number one reason business owners succeed in making massive positive changes in their business as a result of my coaching, is that I ensure they get started and keep going, even when every part of them wants to stop..

Right now, my challenge to you is you must start implementing at least one strategy from this book within 30 minutes of putting it down – that's my challenge to you. Are you up for it?

Where your business will be in 12-months' time will be a direct reflection of implementing the right strategies, in massive amounts, over a consistent period of time.

Consistent, average action always outperforms sporadic brilliance, but to win this race you have to start. Think of the analogy of the hare and the tortoise...

In this chapter I'll give you some of my proven tools to help you on your way, but you must commit to doing the work... are you ready to get going?

The Review Process

The first action I want you to take is to review each of the chapters' action list you should have been filling in as you went along. If you have not done this go back and list the top three actions you are going to take as a direct result of reading each chapter.

I have constructed each chapter to give you enough choice so that you can go back and do this process again when you have finished working through your first list.

So take a moment to put these answers into this final list.

This list will be for your first *100 day SOS Success Plan™*.

My Actions from Each Chapter Are:

Now take a moment to list the top three strategies from this chapter you will implement.

Marketing Chapter 3:

1...

2...

3...

Internet Marketing Chapter 4:

1...

2...

3...

Sales Chapter 5:

1...

2...

3...

Cash flow Chapter 6:

1...

2...

3...

Profit Chapter 7:

1...

2...

3...

Team Chapter 8:

1...

2...

3...

Time Management Chapter 9:

1...

2...

3...

Now rate the top 5 MUST complete actions, the first small step you can take to get them moving and the target date you'll complete them by.

I would love to hear what they are and how you're doing so Post them on the Blog **www.Paul-Avins.com/SOSblog**

You Can't Get a Little Bit Pregnant

As any woman knows, this is true but it also applies to taking the first steps on your plan. You either do it or you don't, there is no such outcome as 'sort of done it'.

Commit now to get pregnant with success!

Now you have your list, work out what is the next step or action you can take to move it forward. even if it is just a 1% move forward. If you move forward every day on every goal plan, you'll have them all completed in the 100 days.

As Zig Ziglar says *"life is a cinch by the inch"*

No more excuses, or reasons as to why you can't take action. Successful people face the same obstacles – they just keep moving forward until they have a breakthrough.

Get 'Hung by the Tongue'

Now you have your plan on paper it's time to share it with somebody in your business or life.

There is something magical about proclaiming to another person what you will be doing, especially if that person is sceptical. Why?

Well, once you tell somebody something like that there is no going back. You know every time you see them or talk to them they're going to ask you how is your Success Plan going?

You have to decide who is going to have the last laugh. You or them?

Build in Strong Accountability – Get a Coach!

We all lead very busy lives today and let key goals or actions slide, even though we have every intention of doing them. The road to failure really is paved with good intentions.

What's the key? Well, you can't use the excuse of not knowing what to do anymore. You have more than enough information in this book to cover that. It's doing what you know, and I'm going to suggest that all top performers in sport and business need help to achieve their goals – even Tiger Woods!

Coaching is a proven model that delivers real results through strong accountability, and by providing a framework to help you through the challenges that will be a part of your journey.

We all need coaches in the different areas of our lives, as learning from others is a far faster way to success than trial and error, as I'm sure you would agree.

Over the last 10 years I've had a number of coaches in different areas of my life, health, business and speaking, to name a few.

If you've not experienced the power of coaching, now is the right time to start. It's important to find a coach you connect with and somebody who you feel will inspire you to the next level in your life.

If you would like me to coach you and your business to success, e-mail to **success@paul-avins.com** or visit **www.paul-avins.com** today.

Celebrate Your Successes

Building a successful business is a journey and
success is not the final destination. In order to
keep your motivation high it's important to break
your big goals down into small steps, but it's even
more important to celebrate your successes along
the way.

Ask yourself:

"How will I celebrate when I achieve ...?"

Perhaps a meal out with your family or friends, perhaps some new
clothes or a weekend away to recharge?

Whatever it is for you, make sure you build in meaningful
celebrations along your journey to success.

Start Documenting the Positive Wins from Each Day

With so much negativity in the media it's easy to get overwhelmed
by the feeling that nothing positive is happening in your business.
The danger in this is that if you focus on what you don't want you
get more of it!

A great success habit to start developing in your life is that of
"journaling" or documenting wins, no matter how small every day.
Then at the end of the week review the small positive steps you've
taken and see what a difference it makes to your attitude.

A Zig Ziglar once said "too many people need a check up from the
neck up" and we must guard our attitude with our lives, because our
business may well depend on it.

Just Keep Swimming

I wanted to finish this chapter with a poem that I have always drawn strength from in challenging times.

I feel it sums up a very underrated entrepreneur's skill that is wonderfully articulated in the great film, *Finding Nemo*. When Dora (the blue fish) says "Just keep Swimming, just keep swimming" whenever they are faced with a setback on the long journey to find Nemo.

PERSISTENCE

Nothing in the world can take the place of persistence

TALENT WILL NOT. . .

Nothing is more common than unsuccessful men with talent.

GENIUS WILL NOT. . .

Unrewarded genius is almost a proverb.

EDUCATION WILL NOT. . .

The world is full of educated derelicts.

PERSISTENCE AND DETERMINATION ALONE ARE OMNIPOTENT.

So...now you have a very strong life ring to keep you and your business afloat. All you have to do is keep swimming and keep learning.

I wish you every success in the future and please keep me informed of what's worked for you on the Blog **www.paul-avins.com/sosblog** the best results each win personal coaching time on their business with me worth up to £500!

Rewarding Your Success

As you'll know from the chapter of building your SOS Action Plan, celebrating success is a very important part of the journey. Yet as entrepreneurs there are very few formal ways we can get recognised fo our achievements. There is a saying about the power of recognition that goes:

"Babies cry for it and soldiers die for it," I would add: entrepreneurs strive for it.

To recognise clients and Wealth Club members who have moved forward with their businesses, each year I hold my Annual Client Appreciation and Awards Dinner.

This is a fun-filled black tie evening where all my clients from the past year get together to celebrate each other's successes, or to draw motivation and inspiration for the following year.

The categories we have recognised over the years include:

- Networker of the Year

- Team of the Year

- PR Personality of the Year

- Marketer of the Year

- Explosive Profit Growth

- Leadership Growth

- Business of the Year.

The 2007 Award Winners

The 2008 Award Winners

To qualify for the awards you must be an active Wealth Club member or have been a coaching client in the last 12 months.

PaUL aVINS
IGNITING BUSINESS RESULTS

My Offer To Business Owners...

FREE ENTRY
(valued at £98) for
up to 2 people with
this voucher

Claim your **2 FREE** tickets to
Paul's Business SOS Seminars

Just go to ↓

Paul-Avins.com/workshop
or call 0845 3707505
to find the seminar nearest to you.

See you there !

Pa

Offer applies in the UK only.

Chapter 11:

The BONUS Strategy

— Building Your Mastermind Network

"The Bigger your Network the Bigger your Net Worth"

— Paul Avins

Being a business owner and entrepreneur can be a very lonely existence, especially in these tough times. After all, who can you talk to about what's happening? You can't talk to your competitors, as they'll exploit it. You can't talk to your suppliers, as they're likely to reduce your credit rating.

If you mention any worries to your bank manager, he may call in your overdraft and as for sharing your concerns with your Partner... well, we both know that's not an option, don't we?

In the legendary book *Think and Grow Rich* by Napoleon Hill, the creation of a Mastermind Group is one of the key strategies he found that very successful people implemented into their lives.

One of my mentors once said that, within 10%, you will earn the average of the ten people you hang around with most! Now, for some of you that's not very motivational, but whatever your current income and whatever you desire it to be, DECIDE to spend more time around more successful people who are heading in the direction you want to go.

I am so committed to this strategy that not only have I joined many mastermind groups over the years, some formal, some informal, I have also launched my own in the form in The Wealth Club which meets every two weeks on a Tuesday morning in Oxford.

The Oxford Wealth Club is based on 3 key concepts:

1. Being part of a supportive Mastermind Group with other successful, business owners just like you.

2. Learning, and remembering, ideas, strategies and skills to take away and implement in your business that week, to grow your profits and wealth.

3. Living in Abundance by helping other business owners, with introductions and referrals to people who they can do business with.

In addition to these regular meetings there are also monthly training sessions and personal coaching time included in the 12-month membership.

Wealth Club Open Days

Paul presenting at a Wealth Club workshop

Business Owners at our May 2009 Open Day

These are special events we run twice a year where we get some of the best business people and speakers in the world to share their strategies for Wealth Creation. It's part of my overall passion to bring the best information to business people just like you to help you speed down the Wealth Highway™. More on this in my forthcoming book, *Turbo Business™*.

We've had some amazing speakers including:

Rachel Elnaugh – Former BBC2 Dragon from Dragons Den

Frank Furness – Sales Expert www.FrankFurness.com

Mike Southon – Author of The Beermat Entrepreneur

Mike Southon with my Team and the OWC Members

Rewarding the top Wealth Lead™ giver – Danny O'Sullivan of Stirling Partners

Andy Shaw & Greg Ballard – Passive Investments

Simon Zutshi – Property Investors Network

OWC Members networking before we begin the meeting

Wealth Club Members exchanging Wealth Leads

11 – The BONUS Strategy — Building Your Mastermind Network

Visitor in the members exhibition area at the May 2009 Open Day

To book your place on the next Open Day go to
www.oxfordwealthclubopenday.co.uk or visit
www.wealth-club.biz it's the right Mastermind Network to take you
to the next level.

Bonus:

2 Free Visits to The Oxford Wealth Club

(valued at £99.00 plus 90-day session worth £200)

WEALTH CLUB

PASSIONATE PEOPLE INSPIRING SUCCESS

Bonus Free Offer

This voucher entitles 1 person to attend
2 x Oxford Wealth Club meetings &
1 x 90 day Planning Session, (valued at £299!)
Free of charge...

 Visit 1 Date:

 Visit 2 Date:

90 Day Session Date:

For a full list of meeting dates visit
www.Wealth-Club.Biz Today !
or call 0845 3707505

Grow your Networth - Build your Networth™

See you there !

Offer applies in the UK only.

www.wealthclubopenday.co.uk

"Helping inspire and coach business
owners to reach new levels
of success is what drives me
every day."

Chapter 12:

Paul's Wealth Club Members Speak Out!

"Since joining the Wealth Club in September 2009 not only have I obtained new business, I have also found a fantastic environment to develop my business with a group of trusted business people. All businesses new and old should consider becoming members.

Mention Business SOS and receive a FREE consultation on current insurance to see if we can match your needs."

— Bryan Baines, Coversure Insurance Services
www.coversure-oxford.co.uk

"Being part of the wealth club means never having that feeling of being alone, where else can you get 50 top flight advisors who want you to succeed!"

— Paul Fowler, Enstone Flying Club
www.enstoneflyingclub.co.uk

"In 'education' it is hard to view what you are doing as a business, but with the serious business implications and responsibilities involved of caring in "loco parentis" for so many little ones, parents, families and over 50 staff in our team, Paul's Wealth Club plays an invaluable part of keeping me sane!..and with such support from the other group members as you would not believe!"

— Valerie Grady BSc. (Hons) P.G.C.E, Willow Cottage Nurseries.
"Second to Mum" childcare and a pre-school education of excellence.
www.willow-cottage.com

"We renewed for our 3rd year at Wealth Club, because it is a fantastic resource for knowledge, energy and business growth – it also pays for itself and our time over and over with the business we do with members and contacts we make over breakfast.

Get Support provide expert Computer Services and Support in plain English and for readers of Business SOS will come to your office, assess your current IT setup and provide a written report on its current state for free. Subject to availability."

— James Craddock MD, Get Support
www.getsupport.co.uk

"Paul Avins and the Oxford Wealth Club have made a huge difference to our thinking and our business in a very short space of time, with practical advice that increased our turnover within 1 week. Nothing to lose and everything to gain.

Mention Business SOS when you book your first computer MOT and we'll give you £25 off."

— Richard Hillsdon, Oxford Home IT Support
www.homeitsupport.biz

"The Oxford Wealth Club is the regular event that keeps me focused, applying initiatives to drive my business forward. It really does get me to raise my game and keep it raised, resulting in more growth, more contacts & more wealth.

Our recession beating offer: £500 plus worth of design is included in all advertising rates for Local Building Matters and Horizons and Futures and you can take it and use it elsewhere."

— Ben Jackson, BBK Media Ltd

"In the last 12 months, Paul's coaching has really helped me to think bigger about my business, my profits are now up over 200% on last year and we are still growing - you can't argue with results like that!"

— Jill Treloggen (MD), Jill Treloggen Interiors
www.jilltreloggeninteriors.com

"As a Sole Trader, The Wealth Club is my team meeting, and a vital part of my business tool kit. Recently, I acted on one easy to use business tip, and brought in enough profit to pay for my membership, from just 1 phone call and 1 transaction! A big thank you to Paul and the team!

10% off our already competitive prices, on all types of window blinds and our huge selection of curtain tracks and poles. Free quotes! Just mention Business SOS when you order."

— Tim Monahan, Fit-ex.com
www.fit-ex.com

"Of all the decisions I made when starting my company, joining the Oxford Wealth Club and having Paul Avins as a coach was one of the very best, with long-lasting beneficial results – which are carrying on even through the recession!

Special Offer: FREE website audit, with recommendations for increased effectiveness (worth £220.00)."

— Sarah Williams, MD, Wordsmith™
www.wordsmithtm.co.uk

"A combination of coaching with Paul and membership of the Wealth Club has given me direction, focus and drive in running my business. How do I know the inspiring motivation and sound advice has worked? I think a 28% increase in turnover in the last 11 months goes some way to show how valuable the experience has been to my life.

Free Cinema vouchers for the whole family! Just try our FREE Family Trial Weeks at any of our 24 clubs"

— Christie Bytom, Bytomic TKD Enriching, Improving
and Empowering Lives through Martial Arts
www.btkd.co.uk

"The energy of the members is evident for the newcomer to see. This is different from a typical networking club with all the businesses helping each other by sharing ideas and experiences – the only question I could ask myself was why wouldn't I want to join?"

— Graham Smith, GSBS
www.GSBS.co.uk.

"I would like to thank Paul and Wealth Club for helping me remember that I shouldn't get engrossed in the day to day activities of running my business but need to take a step out of the daily activities to evaluate and plan my long term goals."

— Julie Farmer, myPA Business Ltd
www.mypabusiness.com

"Paul Avins and his team at The Wealth Club provide sound and practical thought leadership in a caring, sponsored and explorative environment; and that's just over breakfast." PeopleClues™ is a set of leading edge, validated behavioural assessments that measure personality traits, cognitive abilities and attitudes."

For your free trial account please log onto:
www.peopleclues.co.uk/recessionsos

— Davo Ruthven-Stuart, Director, PeopleClues™ UK.

"I have been a member of the Oxford Wealth club for over 3 years. I was sceptical about joining; however, Paul convinced me I would gain new business and education to help me move my business forward. He was right. I have achieved a 1000% return on investment two years in a row and I have made some great contacts.

Can Video help promote your business? To find out see www.aviworks.com and obtain a £25.00 discount (Non Members only) on your next production by quoting Business SOS when enquiring."

— Mario Crispino, B.Eng, AVIWorks Video Productions
www.aviworks.com

"If you need a sounding board to discuss and clarify your business the Wealth Club is the place to go. It has given me the opportunity to move towards working on my business rather than in it. I use it as a resource for business education.

Get 6 months free hosting and two hours of consultation on 'How to make your website work' when you sign up for a Content Management System website. Just mention Business SOS."

— Edward Williams MD, OFEC Consulting Ltd
www.ofec.co.uk

"Paul is knowledgeable, motivational, and willing to share. Oxford Wealth Club is an inspirational networking group of like-minded owners of SMEs. The total value of its individuals and what they offer each other is immeasurable. Three great years."

— Hilary & Harry Fletcher, ECCO shoes Oxford
www.ecco-shoes.co.uk

"The Wealth Club is more of a marketing group than a network group with attitude and passion for all its members and visitors. www.facechart.co.uk was born out of working with other members of the Wealth Club, an excellent result"

— Dave Beesley, B-Line Business Supplies
www.b-line.co.uk

"Paul Avins models the role of inspired leadership. He commands the room with his presence, engages with us directly so we absorb his messages and transforms our business knowledge and ideas so we grow wealthy. All learning and growth happens in a place of uncertainty. With his warmth, humanity and self deprecatory charm, he creates an excitement to develop and grow beyond where we are now, to win business – I shall always remember, "Money loves speed!"

— Sarah McCloughry, "helping business leaders 'talk their walk'"
MD of Anrah Training & Development
www.anrah.co.uk

"The Wealth Club is truly amazing. Paul Avins has developed a culture of abundant thinking where members help one another and share learning. Paul is so creative, inspiring and motivating."

— Heather Salter, Jigsaw HR Limited
www.jigsawhr.com

"I have been in the Wealth Club for three years now; the fact that I keep renewing my membership speaks for itself. Business coaching from Paul plus being in a room full of motivated forward thinking business people is just amazing!

Anyone placing a day's photography with me and quoting Paul's book will receive a 15% discount."

— Neil Ginger, Ginger Photography
www.gingerphoto.co.uk

"The atmosphere at any Wealth Club is always full of positive motivation – a great way to share ideas!

Here's how to identify and control the energy slumps that could be losing you business – 10% OFF The Busy Exec Package"

— Jackie Cross, Life in Balance
www.lifeinbalance.co.uk

"The Wealth Club has been an invaluable and cost effective marketing tool which has helped strengthen and grow my Company. Regular support, encouragement and business development is key to its success.

FREE legal Advice: Getting the right legal advice and information is vital for protecting your business. Arrange a free one hour consultation with Beechwood Solicitors to highlight the important legal issues that affect your business."

— Nicola Stapleton, Beechwood Solicitors
www.beechwoodsolicitors.com

"The Wealth Club has really concentrated my mind on which aspects of my business I need to stay focused on during this recession, and how crucial targeted marketing is to the success of my business."

— Katy Gordon, Co-Creating Balance Ltd

"The Project Managers have been members of Paul's Wealth Club for three years and remain so due to the fresh information, presentation and challenges that Paul brings to every event. It is through his vision we have raised our business expectation to show growth year on year. We offer additional pairs of hands for tasks best outsourced: people, products or processes."

— Peronel Barnes, The Project Managers
www.the-project-managers.com

"The Wealth Club has been a massive boost to our business – I can guarantee that I will leave each meeting with one nugget of information which will help my business, and that is priceless.

B4 Magazine would like to offer 10% discount on all quoted rates for advertising or editorial in B4 Magazine in 2009."

— Richard Rosser, Managing Director, The In Oxford Group Editor,
B4 Business Magazine
www.inoxford.com   www.b4-business.com

"All the networking opportunities you expect from a regular membership group but the magic ingredient in the Wealth Club is Paul Avins – he shares his huge fund of good advice, energy and experience in a range of regular training slots, workshops and coaching opportunities, all included in the membership. The loyalty this generates is amazing and with very good reason."

10% off all consultations when you mention Business SOS."

— Alison Haill, Managing Director of
Oxford Professional Consulting Ltd
www.oxfordprofessionalconsulting.com

"Running a young business can be hard work, thankfully having Paul and his Oxford Wealth Club is a great environment for mental stimulation and regular encouragement. For me our fortnightly meetings are a regular boost of business nutrition and essential learning!

Claim £30.00 off an exclusive tailor-made digital marketing consultation (worth £79.00)."

— Rob Jones, Surefire Digital
www.surefiredigital.co.uk/Business-SOS

"Following Paul's advice we have maintained a positive attitude, increased our marketing activity and implemented many of his recession beating strategies. Enquiries were up over 100% year on year in January with a conversion rate of 60%. February 09 enquiries are up 30% with an 85% conversion rate so far."

— Niall Douglas, Full Circle Travel
www.fullcircletravel.com

"The Oxford Wealth Club has numerous different benefits for its members. From my perspective the business education aspect is truly awesome. OWC makes you think differently and more clearly about your business.

Oxford Management Solutions Ltd would like to offer you 20% off a 1-day intensive strategic review of your business."

— Paul Ovington, Oxford Management Solutions Ltd.
www.oxfordltd.co.uk

"The business skills that Paul has taught me at the Wealth Club have been invaluable to the success and progress of my business over the last 12-months. 'SplashOut' is a Jewellery and fashion accessories retailer supplying on-line at **www.splashoutaccessories.co.uk**.

Join my client database on the site to receive regular offers and discounts."

— Liz Coulter – Wood 'n' Splash

...News Flash
...Wealth Club is expanding!

If you are a passionate Business Coach looking for a great way to attract clients, build a market leading reputation and add a new Profit Stream to your business call us today on 01869 278900 or e-mail **angela@paul-avins.com** to find out how you can open your very own Wealth Club and create raving fans like these!

IGNITING BUSINESS RESULTS

Tel: 0845 3707505

e-mail: p.avins@paul-avins.com

www.Paul-Avins.com

Follow me at

www.twitterpaulavins.com

Connect with me on

www.Facebook.com/paulavins

Blog

www.PaulAvinsBlog.com

PAUL AVINS

5 Reasons to book to speak at your

1. **He knows what he's talking about!** With a 17 year track record of building businesses and coaching success-driven entrepreneurs across the world

2. His proven, powerful, practical strategies **deliver real results**

3. He coaches business owners to **unlock their hidden profits**

4. He delivers presentations on **business growth**, **sales**, **marketing**, and **wealth creation** so you always get the message that is right for your audience

5. His presentations come with a better than **100% money back guarantee**, so you are risk free when you book him

"Paul Avins was my number one choice for talking about how to create and run a successful business at my Weath Workout workshops. The reason is simple: my clients pay a high ticket price and therefore demand the best. Paul adds so much value in the time I give him it is incredible. He is the real thing and it makes me look good to have Paul on board"

— Marcus de Maria, Wealth Coach and Speaker

Paul
next event

Call now on **0845 3707505** to book Paul to speak at your event.
Or go to **www.paul-avins.com**

"Greatness is not in where we stand, but in what direction we are moving. We must sail sometimes with the wind and sometimes against it - but sail we must and not drift, nor lie at anchor."
— Oliver Wendell Holmes

Are you an expert?

Sunmakers can brand your expertise to make it shine

We can make your brand, your website, products, books and ebooks sell for you when you're not there.

We design and publish an eclectic range of books written by leading experts. Perhaps you should be one of them?

SPECIAL OFFER: Get a free brand and product appraisal. Contact us with your details and quote Business SOS.

www.sunmakers.co.uk
+44 (0)1865 779944   twitter.com/BrandingExperts